INTRODUCTION

WHY THIS BOOK

Clear communication is one of the most important aspects of any job. You may need to communicate in writing with a host of people—for instance, your boss, supervisor, coworkers, members, stakeholders, and clients. The purpose of *Professional Writing Skills* is to help you write clearly to all of your readers.

The first edition of this book was published in 1997 by Janis Fisher Chan and Diane Lutovich. While many aspects of the business world have changed since then, clear communication is more important than ever.

E-mail and other electronic forms of communication have made our written communication more frequent, making it increasingly important that business writers deliver focused messages. It's vital to remember that you can never be sure how attentive or how critical your readers are. As business moves faster and faster, the need for clear, error-free communication grows.

ABOUT THIS BOOK

We've designed *Professional Writing Skills: A Write It Well Guide* to provide practical information, ideas, and strategies for improving your business writing.

You'll find this book helpful whether your workplace is a huge corporation or a small business. You can benefit from these writing guidelines whether you work in a professional office, a non-profit organization, an academic institution, or a government agency.

If you write e-mail or any other types of professional documents, the information in this book will help you communicate more effectively, more efficiently, and more professionally. You'll see your writing get better results.

COURSE OBJECTIVES

When you complete this training course, you will be able to:

- Follow a time-tested planning process that will help you think about your reader, purpose, and main point; answer the readers' questions; and organize your information logically

- Write a first draft without a lot of redrafting

- Use concise language that impresses readers with its clarity

- Present a professional image by using correct grammar and punctuation

- Follow e-mail best practices by sending appropriate messages, getting to the point quickly and clearly, and crafting attention-getting subject lines

LESSON OVERVIEWS

Each of the seven lessons includes explanations, examples, questions, and activities that are designed to help you write more effectively and efficiently.

Here's a quick look at what's in the book:

Lesson 1: Develop a Writing Plan in Six Steps
Thoughtful preparation makes any document more effective. Your writing benefits when you put yourself in your readers' shoes, and when you organize the information you present. This lesson outlines six steps to develop a writing plan for e-mail messages, reports, proposals, marketing materials, and more.

Lesson 2: Write the First Draft
The six-step planning method will propel you forward through the first draft of any written communication. In this lesson, you'll learn to present this information, transition from one topic to another, and format your message for the reader.

Lesson 3: Use Concise Language
Long-winded writing can be confusing, and it implies that you do not value your readers' time. This lesson helps you identify and avoid sentence clutter, avoid repetition, and eliminate unnecessary words in your writing.

Lesson 4: Use Clear Language
Your readers may stop paying attention to your documents if they find your language vague or confusing. This lesson helps you write active, specific, straightforward sentences that your readers will grasp easily.

Lesson 5:   **Use Correct Grammar**

Incorrect grammar can reduce your and your organization's credibility. This lesson presents widely accepted and easy-to-use grammar and style guidelines to apply to your business documents.

Lesson 6:   **Use Correct Punctuation**

Incorrect punctuation can give your readers an impression of carelessness. This lesson lays out punctuation rules that many business writers either neglect or have forgotten.

Lesson 7:   **Write Effective E-Mail**

E-mail is a vital way we communicate with coworkers, customers, and clients. Learn how to write clear, concise, appropriate e-mail that quickly conveys the information people need. This lesson will help you convey a consistent professional image and get results from the messages you send.

BEFORE YOU BEGIN

Here are a few things to keep in mind as you work through this book:

USE THE BOOK THE WAY IT WORKS FOR YOU. You might use it as a workbook, scribbling in the margins and using the Notes pages at the end of each lesson to record your own ideas. Or you might use the Table of Contents to jump right to the topic that is of most interest to you.

THINK ABOUT WHAT YOU'RE READING. We've included questions to help you think about the material and suggested ways you can apply what you learn. Twenty-five years' experience working with adult learners helped us create job-relevant exercises and activities.

YOU CAN USE THIS BOOK FOR TRAINING. If you're a manager, human resources professional, trainer, or team leader, you can distribute this book to anyone in your organization who writes for work, or you can use the book as the material for a workshop. (See our website, www.writeitwell.com, for information about our facilitator kits, or contact Write It Well for information about how we'd use the book to deliver a workshop to your staff.)

SCHEDULE TIME TO COMPLETE THE COURSE. If you're going through the book on your own, be sure to schedule time to work on it. Depending on how quickly you work, each lesson will take between 30 and 60 minutes to complete. Turn off your e-mail, close your office door, reserve a conference room, find a quiet space, or do whatever you need to do to focus on reading and completing the exercises and activities in the book. Give yourself a deadline for completing the course. It's best to complete the entire course within four weeks.

MAKE IT JOB-RELEVANT.   As you work through this course you'll be guided through the planning and drafting of your own work-related document, so start thinking about something you need to write. You'll be able to check something off of your to-do list when you've finished this course. Busy professionals learn best by this "learn by doing" approach.

COLLECT WRITING SAMPLES.   Before you begin Lesson 1, collect three samples of your writing. If possible, find samples of writing you've done within the last six months. Your discoveries will inform the way you write in the future.

Let's start by looking at the purpose of business and professional writing.

OVERVIEW

THE PURPOSE OF BUSINESS AND PROFESSIONAL WRITING

Business writing is unique. It is distinguished from other types of writing by its content, its form, and its purpose. For example, the purpose of fiction is to create a world, based on reality or not, in which readers can experience such feelings as fear, amusement, loneliness, suspense, joy, and adventure.

> The great Pullman was whirling onward with such dignity of motion that a glance from the window seemed simply to prove that the plains of Texas were pouring eastward. Vast flats of green grass, dull-hued spaces of mesquite and cactus, groups of frame houses, woods of light and tender trees, all were sweeping into the east over the horizon, a precipice.
>
> from Stephen Crane's short story
> "The Bride Comes to Yellow Sky"

The purpose of an essay is to analyze or interpret a situation.

> A few years ago I wrote a book which dealt in part with the difficulties of the English in India. Feeling that they would have had no difficulties in India themselves, the Americans read the book freely. The more they read it the better it made them feel, and a cheque to the author was the result. I bought a wood with the cheque. It is not a large wood—it contains scarcely any trees, and it is intersected, blast it, by a public footpath. Still, it is the first property that I have owned, so it is right that other people should participate in my shame, and should ask themselves, in accents that will vary in horror, this very important question: What is the effect of property upon the character?
>
> from E. M. Forster's essay "My Wood"

The purpose of personal writing is to express personal experiences, needs, feelings, or expectations.

> Dear Mom,
>
> I'm sorry I forgot your birthday. October came so fast this year—I hadn't even realized summer was over. I hope it was a happy day, and that you were not too hurt when I didn't call.
>
> > Love,
> > Your son

But what is the purpose of business writing? Read the following e-mail, and then briefly describe its purpose.

> TO: Data Processing Managers
> SUBJECT: Delays in Data Processing
>
> There's a problem with the Data Processing group, and as a manager, you can help solve it.
>
> The group has failed to meet its deadlines for the past several months, and this failure is causing delays and confusion throughout the organization. Please take the following steps:
>
> - Make sure your team members read the Data Processing Organizational Format
>
> - Make sure they follow the format and do not duplicate one another's efforts
>
> - Ensure that each member understands the other members' responsibilities so that any one person can fill in for another when needed
>
> When reporting any problems, follow the procedures on page 603 of the Manager's Handbook.
>
> If you have questions or other suggestions, please call.

I think the purpose of this e-mail is _____

_____

_____

The purpose of professional writing is to help people conduct business by providing them with information they need.

To accomplish its purpose, business writing *must* be easy to understand. In fact, the best way to determine whether a business document is well written is to take the reader's point of view. Try that now.

Imagine you are one of the staff members who received this e-mail. Read it and then complete the exercise on the next page.

FROM: Department Manager
TO: Customer Service Staff
SUBJECT: E-Mail Response

We are very fortunate to be in an industry that is expanding. FLEC is the leader in our industry, we are the largest manufacturer of helix type FRT's in the world. There is no reason to be complacent, as the competition is working hard to catch up. We must continue to optimize our opportunities. Again, I want to thank you and keep up the good work.

Customer service will continue to be important and we have received a larger number of e-mails than in prior months. Some of the questions about the product are difficult to answer and I understand that it takes some time to figure out who is the right salesperson for each of the clients. I have heard complaints, however, from customers, that they got an automated response from the system but didn't hear back from a sales rep for almost a week. That is unacceptable because our policy is different. I followed up on a couple of these complaints and it looks like our team has been slow to get the messages to the right sales rep. I know that there is a lot going on, but we have a high work load and need to be as productive as possible.

If you can't find the right rep, you need to come to talk to me about it because we need to improve these numbers. Our customer service guidelines state that anyone who writes should get a personalized message within 24 hours, so let me know if that's a problem. I would like to thank each of you for the extra effort that you have expended as a result of the heavy work load.

EXERCISE

1. State the writer's main point in one sentence.

   ■ _____

   _____

   ☐ I'm not sure what the writer's main point is.

2. Did you have to reread the e-mail to understand what the writer was trying to say?

   ☐ YES   ☐ NO

3. What is your image of the person who wrote this e-mail?

   _____

   _____

   Turn the page for a discussion of the e-mail.

ANSWERS

1. You may have had difficulty identifying the writer's main point—it's not clearly stated, and what is there is buried in the middle of the e-mail.

    Here are two possible main points:

    - ■ "You must connect the customer to their sales rep within 24 hours."
    - ■ "Thanks for your extra effort."

2. It would be very difficult to understand this e-mail without rereading it, and that's a waste of time. Writers are responsible for presenting information so readers only have to read it once.

3. Whatever your image of this writer, it's probably not the image that the writer would like to project. The impression is of someone who is disorganized and unfocused—or who has trouble expressing what he or she wants to say. The writer doesn't seem to have spent much time on the e-mail, implying that it isn't very important. And if it isn't important, why should you bother reading it?

Suppose you were asked to help this writer. Use the space below to list suggestions you would make to help the person write more clearly. The first one is done for you.

This is my advice for the writer:

- • State the main point clearly, right at the beginning _____

_____

_____

CRITERIA FOR EFFECTIVE BUSINESS WRITING

For business writing to be effective, the writer must:

- State the main point clearly, right at the beginning
- Organize information logically
- Leave out unnecessary information
- Use short sentences and paragraphs
- Eliminate unnecessary words
- Include all necessary information
- Use active, precise language and plain English
- Use correct grammar, punctuation, and spelling

Now you have a list of standards for your writing to meet. During this course, you'll learn to develop business writing that meets these standards.

1 DEVELOP A WRITING PLAN IN SIX STEPS

OBJECTIVES

In this lesson, you'll learn six effective steps for planning any professional document.

WHAT YOU NEED

- Two or three samples of your writing

In Lesson 1 of this course, you'll learn a **six-step process** to help you plan your writing logically and efficiently. Each step is carefully designed to move you toward a finished product that says what you want it to say.

Here are the six steps:

1. Think about what you're going to write from the reader's point of view.

2. Decide what you want to accomplish: is your primary purpose to influence readers or to inform them?

3. Compose a key sentence that expresses your most important message.

4. List the facts and ideas that will accomplish your purpose.

5. Group points into categories.

6. Introduce the points you'll make.

Professional writers tend to allocate their time by the percentages in this chart. What do you notice about it?

The Value of Planning

% of Time	Activity
5	Think about readers
5	Think about purpose
5	Identify main point(s)
20	Select information to include
20	Organize information
20	Write quick first draft
20	Revise and edit
5	Proof and correct

You might notice that professional writers spend more time planning their document than they do writing. If you're busy at work, you might think that you don't have time to spend on planning, but planning will save you time later.

As in the following example, we have all read material by writers who lose us at some point in the document—sometimes from the first few words. Read this excerpt:

> Some of the current problems that have been experienced with the current PDCS process/system that have been highlighted are (1) Process/system has become antiquated and inefficient, (2) this means it currently takes 30 minutes to process a claim, this time can be extended substantially in the case that information has been purged from source. (3) Limited reporting functionalities preventing full visibility to past and current claims. The system is in need of updating. Your feedback on this would be appreciated ASAP.

Obviously, this writer didn't take much time to think about what he or she wanted to communicate. What do you think the writer was trying to communicate?

_____

_____

_____

_____

_____

Here's one potential revision:

> Please give us approval to update the PCDS system, which is antiquated and inefficient. An updated system will allow us to streamline claims processing and store documentation so users can access it quickly and easily.

See how much clearer this message is when the writer takes time for planning? What are some of the benefits of planning?

1. —————————————————————————————

2. —————————————————————————————

3. —————————————————————————————

4. —————————————————————————————

5. —————————————————————————————

Turn the page to see some benefits.

Here are some of the benefits you may have listed:

- Fewer miscommunications
- Less time spent clarifying
- Less time spent rewriting
- More positive and more professional image
- Getting the results you want

In the Overview you learned that successful business writing meets specific criteria. In this lesson, you'll learn a step-by-step process to guarantee that your writing meets those criteria. By following this process, you develop a plan for an e-mail, a report, or another document that communicates effectively.

You would never build a house without blueprints. You also need a plan when you write. A writing blueprint makes it possible to get started easily, decide what information to include, and end up with a useful product: a piece of writing your readers can understand easily and quickly.

Now you're ready to start learning the six steps for planning any written communication.

STEP 1.

THINK ABOUT WHAT YOU'RE GOING TO WRITE
FROM YOUR READERS' POINT OF VIEW.

Communication is a two-way process. It takes place when the message you send has been received—and understood—by the person at the other end.

When you're face to face with people, it's easy to know when they aren't getting your message. Furrowed eyebrows, a vacant look, restlessness, questions—all are signs that listeners are confused.

Here's a common situation. Jillian has just started an important project. She will need several key pieces of information from Alan, who works in another division of her company. She sends Alan a detailed e-mail explaining what she needs and when she needs it.

As long as Alan understands her message, he will probably send the information—or at least let her know if he can't.

But what if Jillian's message is confusing? List some ways Jillian might know that Alan did not understand what she meant.

1. _____

2. _____

3. _____

4. _____

If Jillian's message is not clear, Alan might send the wrong information or might not respond at all. Or he might have to call Jillian to ask what she meant. Jillian would have wasted valuable time—hers and Alan's.

Writers sometimes fail to communicate clearly because they haven't stopped to consider their readers. Will readers be interested in the information? Do readers know anything about the subject? Will the message make readers uncomfortable? It's important to answer these kinds of questions before starting to write.

One of the most important steps you can take to increase the chances of a reader's getting your message is to look at what you're writing from the reader's point of view.

Depending on what you're writing, readers may be very interested in the subject, only slightly interested, or not interested at all. They may agree or disagree with your message. They may accept you as an authority on the subject, or they may not have the slightest idea how much expertise you have. They may know as much as you know about the subject, or they may not know anything about it. All these factors can affect their responses.

By thinking about your readers' needs and interests, you can usually identify some predictable reactions before you start writing. Keeping these reactions in mind, you can try to overcome potential resistance, answer questions readers might have, and even increase your credibility.

TRY IT
· · · · · · · · ·

Here are some typical writing situations. Check one that is real and current for you.

I am writing to influence my reader to:

- ■ Adjust my bill

- ■ Correct a problem

- ■ Hire more staff

- ■ Change a procedure

- ■ Other: _____

I am writing to inform my reader about:

- ■ A special assignment I have completed

- ■ A business conference I attended

- ■ The status of a current project

- ■ Other: _____

After you've chosen the situation, write the name of the person who would receive the written communication here. (If you have more than one reader, list their names or describe the group: e.g., "my clients.")

READER'S NAME: _____

Now try to get a clear picture of your reader by asking and answering some of the questions listed below. Add others that you think might be important.

IS THE READER . . .

- Expecting to hear from me?

- Familiar with this subject?

- Already interested in what I have to say?

- Likely to consider me an authority on the subject?

- Likely to find what I have to say useful?

- Familiar with my views on this subject?

- Already committed to a point of view?

- Likely to agree with my point of view?

- Likely to find my message uncomfortable or threatening?

- Other: _____

_____

Never skip this step. Remember, you are writing because you need to communicate something specific to another person or persons. To determine what information to include and to convey that information clearly, you must first focus on your reader(s).

Hint   What if you don't know your reader? Consider what you do know about him or her. Is the person a decision maker? Busy? Likely to receive many e-mails or documents like yours each week? Does the person need your business? A few educated guesses can help you focus even on readers you've never met.

STEP 2.

DECIDE WHAT YOU WANT TO ACCOMPLISH: IS YOUR PRIMARY PURPOSE TO INFLUENCE READERS OR TO INFORM THEM?

To get results, you must clarify exactly what you want to accomplish. Then you will be able to state your most important message clearly.

Your primary purpose for writing always falls into one of two categories: to influence your reader to do something, or to inform your reader about something.

As you read the following e-mail, try to decide whether this writer's primary purpose for writing is to influence his reader or to inform her.

> FROM: Michael Bellows
> TO: Diane Anderson
> SUBJECT: Annual Sales Conference
>
> I would like you to consider moving this year's sales conference to the Horizons Resort Hotel in Marina.
>
> Horizons, which has all the facilities we need, has offered us an excellent package (I've enclosed details). Marina is centrally located and is served by all the major airlines. If we sign a contract by January 15, Horizons will give us an additional ten-percent discount on room rates.
>
> Let me know if you need more information. I'd like to confirm conference plans by the end of next week.

What do you think the primary purpose of this message is?

☐ **INFORM**

☐ **INFLUENCE**

Michael's primary purpose was to influence Diane to do something: move the sales conference to the Horizons Resort Hotel in Marina.

Now read this e-mail and see if you can tell whether the writer's primary purpose is to influence the reader to do something or to inform the reader about something.

> FROM: Eileen McGuigo
> TO: George Blocker
> SUBJECT: Three-Shift Coverage in Processing
>
> For the last several weeks, we have been provided with three-shift coverage in the Processing Department. Company employees have covered the day shift and swing shift. A temporary employee has been covering the night shift. The third shift was covered on a trial basis and is scheduled to end this week. This has been satisfactory and should be continued.

You might have concluded that Eileen's primary purpose was to influence George to keep the temporary worker on the night shift. Perhaps you decided the purpose was to inform George about the way the department has been covered for the last three weeks. Or you may not have been able to identify Eileen's primary purpose.

What would you do if you received that e-mail? You might scan it quickly, and then delete it without hesitating. It has no sense of urgency and no apparent usefulness.

Here's another version of the e-mail. Now can you identify Eileen's primary purpose?

> FROM: Eileen McGuigo
> TO: George Blocker
> SUBJECT: Three-Shift Coverage in Processing
>
> I recommend continuing our three-shift coverage. It has been working out very well in the Processing Department.
>
> By having company employees cover the day and swing shifts and by hiring a temporary employee for the night shift, we have met all our deadlines and made the most efficient use of employees' time.
>
> Please let me know what you decide.

In the second version of the e-mail, you can easily see the writer wants to encourage the reader to continue three-shift coverage in the Processing Department. The primary message is right there in the first paragraph.

AN IMPORTANT REMINDER: You often have more than one purpose when you write. But if the purposes have equal weight, they can end up competing with one another for the reader's attention. It is essential to make one purpose primary.

It's a little like taking photographs. When amateurs use a camera, they often try to get everything and everybody in the frame. The result? A confusing picture in which it's hard to see what the photographer found interesting or worthwhile.

A skilled photographer, on the other hand, makes sure that the most important subject dominates the picture. The viewer's eye is drawn to the subject, no matter how many other people or objects are in the frame.

When you write, help the reader focus on the most important point by determining your primary purpose for writing.

Here are some examples:

> You write primarily to INFLUENCE readers when you write

- an e-mail asking the head office to approve your request for a new computer
- a proposal urging a prospective client to hire your firm for a consulting project

> You write primarily to INFORM readers when you write

- a message to a client explaining the reasons for canceling an insurance policy
- a report detailing the results of a research project

Here are two messages on the same subject. Notice how easy it is to see the writer's purpose in each message.

EXAMPLE 1: Influence the reader to agree to be the keynote speaker

Dear Ms. Layton:

I know you are very busy, but we would be delighted if you would agree to be the Keynote Speaker at the first meeting of Mountain Climbers Anonymous.

Our members would love hearing about your struggles with the obsession to scale great heights. I know your experience and perspectives will be of great value to us.

The meeting will be held on Thursday, October 11, at 6:30 p.m. at the Tiptop Cafe. Please let me know by August 31 whether you will be available to speak.

EXAMPLE 2: Inform readers about the first meeting

Dear Mr. Williams:

The first meeting of Mountain Climbers Anonymous will be held on Thursday, October 11, at 6:30 p.m. at the Tiptop Cafe.

Our Keynote Speaker will be Ms. Marybeth Layton, who will share with us her own struggle to overcome the obsession to scale great heights.

If you plan to attend, we need your reservation form by September 16 so we can order dinner. We hope to see you at the meeting.

PRACTICE

Read each message and identify its primary purpose.

Alicia—

I'd like to suggest that you prepare and distribute an agenda several days before each monthly meeting.

Without an agenda, people waste time coming to meetings they really don't have to attend. Also, people come unprepared to discuss issues because they don't know in advance what will be covered.

I'll be glad to help in any way I can—just let me know.

PRIMARY PURPOSE: ☐ INFLUENCE   ☐ INFORM

TO: Planning Committee Members
RE: Monthly Planning Meeting, August 12

Here's the agenda for our next meeting. I've listed the issues we're discussing so you can come prepared.

If you're not involved in any of the areas on the agenda, you may skip this meeting, but please call me if you do not plan to attend.

PRIMARY PURPOSE: ☐ INFLUENCE   ☐ INFORM

ANSWERS

Alicia—

I'd like to suggest that you prepare and distribute an agenda several days before each monthly meeting.

Without an agenda, people waste time coming to meetings they really don't have to attend. Also, people come unprepared to discuss issues because they don't know in advance what will be covered.

I'll be glad to help in any way I can—just let me know.

PRIMARY PURPOSE: ☒ **INFLUENCE**   ☐ **INFORM**

The writer's primary purpose is to influence Alicia to prepare and distribute an agenda before the monthly meetings.

TO: Planning Committee Members
RE: Monthly Planning Meeting, August 12

Here's the agenda for our next meeting. I've listed the issues we're discussing so you can come prepared.

If you're not involved in any of the areas on the agenda, you may skip this meeting, but please call me if you do not plan to attend.

PRIMARY PURPOSE: ☐ **INFLUENCE**   ☒ **INFORM**

The writer's primary purpose is to inform committee members of the agenda for the meeting.

The purpose is clear in these e-mails because the writers took the time to decide whether they wanted to influence or to inform readers.

Assignment

Look at your own writing. Read each sample and decide if your primary purpose was to influence readers to do something, or to inform them about something.

Do you think your purpose was clear to your readers? If not, make a mental note to determine your primary purpose the next time you write.

TRY IT
. . . .

Here are some typical writing situations. Check one that is real and current for you.

I am writing to influence my reader to:

- Adjust my bill

- Correct a problem

- Hire more staff

- Change a procedure

- Other: _____

I am writing to inform my reader about:

- A special assignment I have completed

- A business conference I attended

- The status of a current project

- Other: _____

STEP 3.

COMPOSE A KEY SENTENCE THAT EXPRESSES
YOUR MOST IMPORTANT MESSAGE.

Think of your key sentence as the one you'd shout if you had three seconds to get your most important message across to someone driving by.

In a well-written document, the sentence carrying the most important message should be so clear that the reader can easily identify it.

Which of the documents below has a clear key sentence?

DOCUMENT A

Dear Mr. Weller:

Safety is our number-one concern and our safety record shows that we are all trained well. There is a lot of traffic on the block of Jefferson Street between South Main and Mission. The street sees heavy traffic very regularly, yet its current condition is a safety hazard. The street should probably be widened. That would have tremendous benefits and we can get the job done. A night permit would allow us to start right away.

DOCUMENT B

Dear Mr. Weller:

My construction company is asking for a noise permit to allow night work on the block of Jefferson Street between South Main and Mission. The street sees heavy traffic very regularly, yet its current condition is a safety hazard.

Widening the street would have tremendous benefits, and we are ready to work day and night to make the necessary repairs.

We hope to begin work as soon as possible. If you have any questions, please contact me at my office.

The key sentence in Document B jumps right out, doesn't it? All key sentences should be this easy to find:

> Dear Mr. Weller:
>
> **My construction company is asking for a noise permit to allow night work on the block of Jefferson Street between South Main and Mission.** The street sees heavy traffic very regularly, yet its current condition is a safety hazard.

But what about Document A? The purpose is obviously to influence, but the message has no clear key sentence, leaving it up to the reader to figure out what the writer wants him or her to do. That document may not get results.

Writers often fail to include a clear key sentence because they either

- haven't decided what they want to say
- hesitate to state their main point directly

But readers are busy people. They don't have time to guess what you mean to say. It is your job to express your most important message clearly. You must be willing to take the time to compose a key sentence that is clear and complete.

EXAMPLES OF KEY SENTENCES

WRITING TO INFLUENCE

I want my reader to do something:

- Give me a 20 percent raise
- Reduce your fee by half
- Build a swimming pool at the new facility

WRITING TO INFORM

I want my reader to know something:

- The project I'm coordinating will be finished by May 19
- I am sorry to tell you that your application for a loan has been denied
- The needs assessment we conducted indicates that two-thirds of your staff would benefit from writing skills training

In the Active Language section of Lesson 4: Use Clear Language, you'll learn how to develop key sentences that are more engaging, direct, and strong.

It is important to include your most important message, but more importantly, you must express this main point as specifically and directly as possible.

In each situation below, the writer wants to influence the reader to do something. For each situation, write a key sentence that says clearly what the writer wants the reader to do. Feel free to invent information if you need to.

SITUATION: Employees are parking in the visitor lot instead of the employee lot, taking up all the spaces reserved for clients.

_____

_____

_____

_____

_____

SITUATION: You collect timecards on the first Friday of the month for the work completed for the prior month. About half of the contractors send the reports about a week late, and you can't bill the client until all the reports are in. The policy is that contract workers can't get paid until the client has been billed. If people sent the report in on time, your manager wouldn't be calling you all the time and the accounting office would be able to manage project billing much better.

_____

_____

_____

_____

_____

Your key sentences probably resemble these. If yours are very different, be sure they clearly express what the writer wants the reader to do.

> All employees should park in the employees' lot instead of the visitors' lot.

> To get paid for your work last month, you must complete your timecards by Friday.

Clear key sentences make it much more likely that your writing will get results. The key sentences you just composed were for situations where the writers want to influence readers to do something. Key sentences read a little differently when your primary purpose is to inform readers about something.

Read the example below. Find and underline the key sentence or most important message in the following example.

PRIMARY PURPOSE: TO INFORM

> TO: Staff

> RE: Holiday Party

> The Holiday Party will be held on December 16 at the Redwood Lodge from noon to 5:00 p.m.

> The sign-up sheet will be posted in the cafeteria by Friday. This year, we're asking everyone to bring a few cans of food for the food drive instead of gifts.

> If you have questions, please call Miriam Belladora at Extension 403. We hope you and your family can attend.

Did you underline the first sentence in the message? If so, you found the key sentence.

Notice that when you're writing to inform, your key sentence or most important message may actually be a statement of one to three sentences, as shown in the example.

PRIMARY PURPOSE: TO INFORM

Dear Clients:

On June 15, I am beginning a three-month leave. While I'm away, my associate, Annabel Leong, will be managing my projects.

Before I leave, Annabel and I will do the following to make sure that everything runs smoothly:

- We will review the status of all projects and meet with the project teams.

- During the last two weeks of May, Annabel will call each of you to introduce herself and answer any questions you may have.

- I will provide Annabel with all the project files so she can answer questions and resolve any problems that might come up.

I've enclosed Annabel's contact info. You can reach her by phone or e-mail.

I look forward to working with you again when I return in September.

PRACTICE

If you have your own writing samples, take them out now. Read each sample and underline your key sentence: the one that tells the reader precisely what to do or what to know.

If you cannot find a key sentence, compose one. Promise yourself to include a clear key sentence the next time you write.

NOTE If you're writing to inform, keep in mind that your key sentence may actually be a two- or three-sentence statement.

Hint You have probably noticed that there is a close relationship between the key sentence and the primary writing purpose. If you have trouble composing a key sentence, ask yourself if you have really decided whether your primary purpose is to influence or to inform.

EXERCISE

For this assignment, complete the first part of a writing plan for a current writing situation of your own. Do the following:

1. Think of an e-mail, message, or short report you need to write. If nothing comes to mind, consider one of these topics:

   ■ Convince your lawyer, doctor, accountant, etc., to reduce his or her fees for a specific service or visit

   ■ Encourage your manager to make a particular purchase for your department

   ■ Suggest a change in the way a procedure is carried out at your place of work

2. Now, go to page 91 and use one of the Writing Worksheets. Notice that the Worksheet includes all six steps of the writing process. For this assignment, however, complete only Steps 1, 2, and 3.

Now you've learned the first three steps to take when you write: consider your readers' point of view, decide what you want to accomplish, and state your main point clearly.

Next you'll learn the rest of the planning process:

   ■ Select the information to include

   ■ Organize information logically

By the time you've finished Steps 1, 2, and 3 of your writing plan, you've gone a long way toward making sure your writing communicates clearly and effectively.

You have a pretty good idea about how readers are likely to respond to your message. You know whether your primary purpose is to influence readers or to inform them. And you have already put your most important message into words—what you want your readers to do or to know.

The steps you'll learn now will take you through the processes of selecting the right information to influence or inform readers, and organizing that information so readers can follow your points easily.

When you have completed all six steps of the writing plan, you will have a logical, effective structure for the specific piece you are writing. Moving from plan to first draft will be easy. You won't have to think about how to get started, or what you want to say, or how you should organize your facts and ideas. You will have taken those steps already.

EXAMPLE

SITUATION: The writer, Sue, knows someone who would be perfect for the position of administrator in her friend Pete Starkey's company. Sue knows Pete has been swamped with applications, and she really wants him to consider her colleague.

Here are Steps 1 through 3 of Sue's writing plan:

1. Sue looks at what she's going to write from her readers' point of view:

    > Pete is not expecting to hear from Sue, considers her knowledgeable, needs the information, and is very busy. He is anxious to fill the position, and wants to interview only three candidates.

2. Sue knows that her primary purpose is to influence Pete.

3. Sue composes a key sentence that expresses what she wants Pete to do:

    > "Hire Gail Schacter to fill the new administrative position in your company."

4. Sue lists the facts and ideas to accomplish her purpose—all the reasons she can think of to answer Pete's obvious question, "Why should I hire Gail Schacter?"

- leader
- strong team member
- self-starter
- friendly
- good sense of humor
- communicates clearly
- finishes what she starts
- gives credit where due
- represents company well
- high management potential
- attentive to detail
- reports are accurate
- tactful
- encourages others to do their best
- conscientious
- sensitive
- does not need to be told what to do
- revised procedures manuals on her own
- never loses sight of big picture

5. Sue groups the points on her list into categories and decides what information belongs in which category. She comes up with five categories, or **key points:**

   - high management potential

   - conscientious

   - strong team member

   - self-starter

   - represents company well

6. Sue writes a summary sentence for each key point and puts the sentences in the order she thinks will be most effective. Under each sentence, she lists the points she plans to include in that category.

   Pete should hire Sue's friend because:
   >   She has high management potential
   >   — leader
   >   — communicates clearly
   >   — never loses sight of big picture
   >   She is a self-starter
   >   — does not need to be told what to do
   >   — revised procedures manual on her own
   >   She is conscientious
   >   — attentive to detail
   >   — reports are accurate
   >   — finishes what she starts
   >   She is a strong team member
   >   — gives credit where due
   >   — encourages others to do their best
   >   She represents the company well
   >   — tactful
   >   — friendly
   >   — sensitive
   >   — good sense of humor

   On the next page you will see the e-mail that Sue wrote.

Notice that Sue only had to add an opening, a few transitions, and a closing to transform her writing plan into a finished message.

Dear Pete:

I heard that you're trying to fill the new administrative position in your department. Look no further—I have the perfect person for the job. **I strongly recommend that you hire my colleague, Gail Schacter.**

I have always felt that **Gail has high management potential.** A strong leader who communicates clearly, she never loses sight of the big picture. Those are qualities the person you hire needs to have.

Gail has shown herself to be a true self-starter who needs little direction. She finds out what needs doing and gets it done. We were very pleased by the way she took it upon herself to revise our outdated procedures manual; the manual now serves as a model for other departments.

You'll quickly discover that **Gail is very conscientious.** She is attentive to detail and her reports are always accurate because she takes the time to check her facts carefully. I have noticed that once she starts a project, she stays with it until it is completed to her satisfaction.

Another of Gail's attributes should be of particular interest to you: **she's a very strong team member.** Time after time I have seen her encourage others to do their best, and she is always quick to give credit where credit is due.

Finally, because the position requires working with the public, you'll want to know that **Gail represents the company well.** Tactful, friendly, and sensitive to others, she also has a great sense of humor—and knows when to use it.

I've enclosed Gail's resume and urge you to give her your serious consideration. She'd be a valuable addition to your staff.

At the end of this lesson, you'll practice these steps by developing a writing plan for a situation of your own.

STEP 4.

LIST THE FACTS AND IDEAS THAT WILL ACCOMPLISH YOUR PURPOSE.

When you start to write something, you usually have a general idea about what information to include. But you still have to determine exactly what facts and ideas readers need to hear before they may feel convinced, or fully informed.

Start by writing down every fact or idea that might influence or inform your readers. This is a brainstorming process, similar to the one you've probably used with your team to come up with creative solutions to problems.

The key is giving yourself permission to write down every point that comes to mind when you ask yourself two basic questions:

> **WRITING TO INFLUENCE**
> WHY should readers do what I want them to do?

> **WRITING TO INFORM**
> WHAT do readers need to know?

At this stage of the planning process, it's very important to write quickly without blocking the flow of ideas by evaluating items on your list. In Step 5, you'll decide which items to keep and which to throw out.

PRACTICE

Try this process yourself with a simple practice situation for Steps 1–4. Imagine that you're an auto dealer replying to an e-mail with a question from a young couple. They don't know much about cars, and would like to buy their first new car.

You've met with them once and know that they care about fuel efficiency, want a car with an integrated hands-free phone device, and that the young man injured his back and wants a car with a very comfortable front seat. You think one model at your dealership might be perfect for them. Their e-mail gives you a chance to write back and tell them why.

STEPS 1–3

1. Look at what you're going to write from your readers' point of view. In this case, imagine you're the salesperson, but put yourself in the readers' shoes. Here's a list of questions you should consider before you write anything.

ARE THE READERS . . .

- expecting to hear from you?
- familiar with the subject?
- already interested in what you have to say?
- likely to consider you an authority on the subject?
- likely to find what you have to say useful?

- familiar with your views on the subject?
- already committed to a point of view?
- likely to agree with your point of view?
- likely to find your message uncomfortable?

2. Decide what you want to accomplish:

- **INFLUENCE** the readers to buy the car, OR
- **INFORM** the readers about the car's features

In this situation, there is definitely something you want your reader to do—buy the car. So it's more effective if your primary purpose is to influence your reader.

3. Compose a key sentence that says exactly what you want the reader to do:

I want my reader to _____

Hint Your key sentence should clearly state what you want your reader to do: "You should consider buying model _____ from our dealership."

Step 4 of the Practice is on the next page.

STEP 4

4.   List the facts and ideas that will accomplish your purpose.

Now you're ready to collect information that will influence your reader to buy the car from you. Remember to keep your readers' point of view in mind and look for points that will be of direct interest to them.

Which of the following thoughts are likely to be influential? Put an **X** beside each thought that might *not* sway the reader.

- ☐ "The model includes the Bluetooth hands-free cellphone link I remember they mentioned."

- ☐ "This model gets excellent mileage."

- ☐ "I want to sell more cars this month than another coworker."

- ☐ "This model's seats are unusually comfortable."

- ☐ "It is inside the price range they mentioned."

- ☐ "This is one of our more expensive models."

- ☐ "They would be safer in this model than the cars made by another company they mentioned when I met them."

If you put an **X** beside "This is one of our more expensive models" and "I want to sell more cars this month than another coworker," you're correct. Those two statements may be true, but the dealership's profit and the salesperson's personal competitiveness are not likely to encourage the potential buyers to do what the salesperson wants.

A new Practice begins on the next page.

PRACTICE

Think of something you want to convince or influence someone to do. Write down your idea

here: _____

Now write down all the reasons it will benefit them or their organization:

1. _____

2. _____

3. _____

4. _____

5. _____

In the next step—Step 5—you're going to practice grouping your ideas into categories.

STEP 5.

GROUP POINTS INTO CATEGORIES.

Whenever you write anything longer than a few sentences, it is important to organize your facts and ideas by grouping them into categories. These categories provide the reader with a road map—a route through the information.

Grouping is a way of organizing information to help people understand it. For example, look at how people learn long-distance phone numbers. Try learning this number:

5135553938

Hard, isn't it? But the number is much easier to learn if it's broken down into groups:

Area Code	Prefix	Number
(513)	555-	3938

In the same way, you can help your readers understand what you have to say by grouping information into related topics.

Grouping points during the planning process also makes writing easier because you don't have to worry about where to begin paragraphs. As you'll see, each group, or topic, usually forms one paragraph.

There is no standard way to organize information. It is a highly individual process that emerges from the situation and your own unique perceptions of what things have in common.

TRY IT
. . . . . .

Can you name a trait that the three items in each of these groups have in common?

Group A	Group B
hammers	paper clips
nails	staples
paint	white-out

You may have noted that the items in Group A are supplies you could get in a hardware store, while those in Group B are office supplies.

You could also regroup the items this way:

Group A	Group B
paint	hammers
white-out	nails
	paper clips
	staples

Now the items in Group A are things you wouldn't want to spill, while the items in Group B are solid tools.

The grouping of facts and ideas is your organizational scheme. The scheme you use depends mostly on the types of information you need to organize, and what you want to accomplish by writing.

The organizational scheme is more useful than a conventional outline because it lets the information determine the organization. In a conventional outline, you tend to start with the categories before you know what information you'll include. It's like forcing your family to fit a house that already exists, rather than letting the size and needs of your family determine the size and layout of the house you build.

Here are some typical organizational schemes:

TOPICS: Suppose you are providing readers with details about three computer systems. You might group information into these categories:

> cost
> size
> special features

CHRONOLOGICAL ORDER: Use this way of grouping information when you want to show events or actions over time. For instance, you might use either of these organizational schemes to present information about a long-term research project:

Scheme 1	Scheme 2
first year	past history
second year	present status
third year	projection for future

COMPARISON AND CONTRAST: Sometimes it's most effective to organize information into two categories and compare them. You might use one of these schemes to give managers details for evaluating whether a particular building is suitable for your company's new offices:

Scheme 1:	pros/cons
Scheme 2:	advantages/disadvantages
Scheme 3:	meets/fails to meet our criteria

You could also consider organizing topics by department, priority, or date needed. There is no right or wrong way to organize information; the important point is that you've developed an organizational scheme that works.

PRACTICE

Here's a list of different foods. Imagine you're writing a report or magazine article about these foods, and organize them into two or three logical groups.

chocolate ice cream	sweet-and-sour pork
spaghetti	strawberries
hamburgers	artichokes
spare ribs	pecan pie
cheese Danish	roast turkey
crab	walnut torte

Here are some ways of grouping the foods on the list. You may have grouped them differently. It's only important that you found some logical organizational scheme.

CHRONOLOGICAL ORDER

Main Courses	Fruits and Vegetables	Desserts
sweet-and-sour pork	artichokes	chocolate ice cream
spaghetti	strawberries	cheese Danish
roast turkey		pecan pie
hamburgers		walnut torte
spare ribs		
crab		

TOPICS

High in Vitamins	High in Protein	High in Starch
strawberries	chocolate ice cream	spaghetti
artichokes	hamburgers	cheese Danish
	spare ribs	pecan pie
	crab	walnut torte
	sweet-and-sour pork	
	roast turkey	

COMPARISON & CONTRAST—PROS & CONS

Foods I Like	Foods I Dislike
chocolate ice cream	hamburgers
cheese Danish	pecan pie
roast turkey	artichokes
spare ribs	spaghetti
sweet-and-sour pork	walnut torte
strawberries	
crab	

Suppose you are writing a magazine article about these athletic activities:

surfing	swimming	volleyball
skiing	scuba diving	baseball
wind surfing	football	mountain climbing
snowboarding	basketball	rock climbing
mountain biking	canoeing	kayaking
rollerblading	tennis	jogging

Here's one way you might organize them:

Water-Related	**Not Water-Related**	
surfing	basketball	rollerblading
canoeing	skiing	rock climbing
wind surfing	tennis	football
swimming	volleyball	jogging
scuba diving	baseball	snowboarding
kayaking	mountain climbing	
	mountain biking	

Now you try it. Organize the activities another way:

Here is one way you might have grouped the activities:

Little or No Cost	Moderately Expensive	Costly
swimming	surfing	canoeing
football	tennis	skiing
basketball	mountain climbing	scuba diving
volleyball	rock climbing	mountain biking
baseball	rollerblading	wind surfing
jogging		snowboarding
		kayaking

Now you've completed Step 5—organizing the points you're going to cover. Next, you'll learn how to introduce these points.

STEP 6.

INTRODUCE THE POINTS YOU'LL MAKE.

Earlier, you learned that each category of information will usually form one paragraph when you write your draft. To guide your readers through your paragraphs, it helps if they have signposts for the main groupings of ideas you set out in your writing.

Summary sentences and introductions to lists are two kinds of signposts you can plant in your writing to show your readers the way forward. Each of them gives readers a heads-up for what they're about to encounter in the text.

SUMMARY SENTENCES

The summary sentence—also known as a paragraph's topic sentence or introductory sentence—expands a category into a statement that introduces the paragraph's central topic, and tells readers why the topic is important. The summary sentence provides a context for the paragraph. Without this context, readers might have trouble following your points, or they might miss important points altogether.

To write a summary sentence when you are writing primarily to *influence* the reader, simply expand the category heading into a statement that directly answers the reader's question, "Why should I do what you want me to do?" (We'll discuss writing summary sentences when your primary purpose is to *inform* later in this section.)

Here's a hypothetical situation to illustrate the process.

> **SITUATION**: Jason wants to influence his manager, Sarah, to authorize the purchase of database software for his department.
>
> Jason knows Sarah's question will be, "Why should I authorize this purchase?" To answer the question, he came up with these points about the software:

- It's easier and faster to search and sort a database than a spreadsheet
- It will save the company money in the long run
- It will help me be more productive
- Production delays have been increasing
- More deadlines have been missed
- I need to import e-mail addresses to my documents quickly
- I need colleagues to help with mailing lists and project plans

Here's how Jason grouped these points:

CATEGORY   **Production Delays**

- There have been long delays and missed deadlines this year because information is scattered across different company departments
- This scattered information takes too long to locate

CATEGORY   **Increased Workload**

- Work will be streamlined and faster as coworkers pool information

CATEGORY   **Save $$**

- I'll be more productive when I search for data, assemble mailing lists, and plan projects

To complete his writing plan, Jason developed a summary sentence for each category by adding a few words to the category heading.

Jason's Writing Plan

Jason believes that Sarah should authorize the purchase of database software for his department because of the factors grouped under the following three headings:

Production Delays

- We are experiencing too many production delays
- We have missed several deadlines this year after delays of five days or more
- Materials were often late because they were hard to find, being scattered across different programs

Increased Workload

- Our workload continues to increase
- It would go faster as coworkers pooled information in a single database

Save $$

- A system of our own will more than pay for itself
- I'll be more productive as I search for information
- I'll be able to get needed information from others immediately for mailing lists and project plans

Turn the page to see the finished e-mail Jason wrote.

Here's how the writing plan provides the logical structure for the e-mail. Notice how the summary sentences start each paragraph.

TO: Sarah
FROM: Jason
RE: Database Software

Sarah,

As we discussed last week, I think it's very important for you to **authorize the purchase of database software** for my department.

Since the reorganization, **we have been experiencing far too many production delays.** In fact, so many departments are using the production facilities that delays of five days or more have become routine. We've been unable to meet several deadlines this year because our materials weren't ready on time. We were hunting for information that should be in one central, easy-to-find location.

This problem continues to get worse because **our workload continues to increase.** I'm now responsible for more project planning and e-mail blasts than ever before.

My calculations show that **a database program of our own will more than pay for itself within six months.** The database will sync with my e-mail program so that from now on, I won't have to enter contacts' addresses twice. And the information I need for projects and mailings will be available immediately over the local area network. I won't need to spend more time asking other people to hunt down the information I need.

Please let me know if you need more information about the benefits of this purchase. Otherwise, I'll stop by on Friday to see what decision you've made.

Thanks,

Jason

INTRODUCTION TO LISTS

Instead of presenting your information in a series of paragraphs with summary sentences, you might present the information in a list with bullet points. In that case, develop an introductory statement to introduce the bulleted points to come. By reading the introductory sentence, the reader will know if the information is important to them and will either continue reading the bulleted list items or continue skimming down the page or screen to the next introductory statement. For guidelines for using lists, turn to page 73.

PRACTICE

Here's an exercise with a new situation to help you practice all six steps.

> **SITUATION**: Your employees' group wants to convince your CEO to provide an in-house exercise facility. As the group's representative, you need to draft an e-mail asking the CEO to allocate funds for the facility.

Steps 1–5 of the writing plan have been completed for you. Read them, and then complete Step 6.

1. Look at what you're going to write **from your readers' point of view.**

    - The CEO is not expecting to hear from me.

    - She is familiar with the employees' desire for this facility.

    - She may be reluctant to spend money.

2. Decide what you want to accomplish.
    In this situation, you definitely want to **influence** your reader.

3. Compose **a key sentence** that expresses your most important message.
    "Please allocate funds for an in-house exercise facility for employees."

4. Make **a list of the facts and ideas** that will accomplish your purpose.
    The CEO should allocate funds for an exercise facility because of these benefits:

    - Saves money—less absenteeism because people who exercise are less likely to get sick

    - Shows company cares about employees

    - Better team spirit when people work out together

    - Reduces cost of health insurance—healthy people have fewer claims

    - Gives people something to look forward to—happier

    - Would be one of first companies in area to invest in exercise facility rather than expect employees to go to outside gyms

Steps 5 and 6 of the Practice are on the next page.

5. Group points into **categories.**

MORALE

- Better team spirit when employees work out together

- Gives people something to look forward to—happier

FINANCIAL

- Saves money—less absenteeism because people who exercise are less likely to get sick

- Reduces cost of health insurance—healthy people have fewer claims

REPUTATION

- Shows company cares about employees

- Would be one of first companies in area to invest in its own exercise facility

Now that you've seen Steps 1–5 in action, complete the Practice by writing out summary sentences in Step 6:

6. **Introduce the points you'll make.**

To complete Step 6, write a summary sentence for each of the three categories from Step 5: "Morale," "Financial," and "Reputation." Remember, in this situation you are writing to influence. So the summary sentence should directly answer the question, "Why should my reader do what I want him or her to do?"

Here are the categories from Step 5. For each category, write one complete sentence that directly answers the question, "Why should the CEO allocate funds for an exercise facility?"

MORALE

- Better team spirit when people work out together

- Gives people something to look forward to—happier

SUMMARY SENTENCE: _____

_____

_____

Step 6 of the Practice continues on the next page.

FINANCIAL

- Saves money—less absenteeism because people who exercise are less likely to get sick

- Reduces cost of health insurance—healthy people have fewer claims

SUMMARY SENTENCE: _____

_____

_____

_____

REPUTATION

- Shows company cares about employees

- Would be one of the first companies in area to invest in exercise facility

SUMMARY SENTENCE: _____

_____

_____

_____

Check your answers for Step 6 on the next page.

ANSWERS

Here are examples of the kinds of summary sentences you may have written.

Your sentences are probably a little different, and they may be very different. That's fine.

The important point is that each sentence should directly answer the question, "Why should the CEO allocate funds for an exercise facility?"

MORALE

EXAMPLE   An exercise facility will improve employee morale.

EXAMPLE   Exercise is good for morale.

FINANCIAL

EXAMPLE   The company would save money by installing an exercise facility.

EXAMPLE   Exercise facilities can save the company money.

REPUTATION

EXAMPLE   Building an exercise facility would do wonders for the company's reputation.

EXAMPLE   Exercise facilities will help give us a positive image.

THERE'S ONLY ONE THING LEFT TO DO.   You now have a complete writing plan for the e-mail to the CEO. The only remaining step is to decide on the best order for the summary sentences.

When determining what information goes first, second, and so on, consider this: pick the summary sentence that your reader is likely to consider the most important, and put that sentence first.

When people read quickly, they tend to pick up beginnings and endings. By putting the most important point first, you increase your chances of catching and keeping your reader's attention.

Sometimes you can put your second-most-important point last. Sometimes, the information dictates some other order.

Look at the summary sentences below. Which point do you think is most likely to convince the CEO to allocate funds for an exercise facility? Number the sentences in the order you think would be best.

_____ An exercise facility will help give us a positive image.

_____ An exercise facility can save the company money.

_____ An exercise facility will improve employee morale.

Here's the order one writer chose, based on the assumption that saving money was likely to be the most important concern to her company's CEO:

1. An exercise facility can save the company money.

2. An exercise facility will help give us a positive image.

3. An exercise facility will improve employee morale.

COMPLETED WRITING PLAN

Here is an example of the writing plan. Notice the way it creates a blueprint for the entire e-mail.

READER:	CEO
PURPOSE:	To influence
KEY SENTENCE:	Our employees' group would like you to allocate funds for an in-house exercise facility.

MAIN POINTS:

1. Exercise facilities can save the company money.
   - Less absenteeism because people who exercise are less likely to get sick
   - Reduced cost of health insurance—healthy people have fewer claims

2. Exercise facilities will help give us a positive image.
   - A way to show that the company cares about employees
   - Would be one of the first companies in area to invest in such a facility

3. An exercise facility will improve employee morale.
   - Increase team spirit by working out together
   - Give people something to look forward to—happier

FINISHED E-MAIL

Notice that the most important message is up front in the first paragraph, and the structure of the e-mail comes directly from the writing plan.

TO: Anna Harbin
FROM: Acme Employees' Association
RE: Exercise Facility

Anna,

After some months of discussion about ways to improve our working environment, we've decided that we'd like you to allocate funds for an in-house exercise facility.

Our research on this topic makes it clear that exercise facilities can save companies money. For instance, people who exercise are less likely to get sick, which means that less money is lost to absenteeism. Also, healthy employees have fewer insurance claims, thus reducing health insurance costs.

An exercise facility will help give us the positive image we are constantly seeking by demonstrating that the company cares about its employees. We have the opportunity to become known as one of the first companies in the area to invest in such a facility.

We also believe that an exercise facility will improve our employees' morale. Working out together is a great way to increase team spirit. People also say they would be happier if they had an exercise session to look forward to at lunch or after work, and that it's a hassle to drive to the local gym after work.

We've enclosed a summary of the facts we collected; we think you'll find them convincing. Please let us know if you need more information. Thanks for considering this request.

WRITING TO INFORM

So far, we've looked at examples of the planning process when the purpose is to influence.

When you write primarily to inform, the process changes slightly. Instead of asking, "*Why* should readers do what I want them to do?" ask, "*What* do readers need to know?" It's your answers to that question that make up the list of facts and ideas to include.

Here's an example.

SITUATION: Joan Huang is in charge of the conference "Newest Trends in Evaluating Performance." She wants everyone in her department to know what will be covered during the conference and how to make arrangements to attend.

READERS: Joan's staff

PURPOSE: To inform

KEY SENTENCE: Here is the current information on the upcoming conference, "Newest Trends in Evaluating Performance."

Joan asks, "What does my staff need to know?" and lists these questions:

- What will be covered at the conference?

- Who will be speaking?

- Where will it be held?

- Dates and times?

- What if I can't attend?

- How and where do I sign up?

- Who is responsible for travel and housing arrangements?

- Who's paying the airfare and hotel expenses?

Next, Joan answers the questions:

- **What will be covered at the conference?**
  - Newest computer-based appraisal systems being tested in the U.S., U.K., and Japan
  - Case studies: 360° feedback
  - Peer evaluations
  - Training methods

- **Who will be speaking?**
  - Representatives from National Institute of Performance
  - Representatives of the National Human Resources Organization
  - Executives from leading European organizations
  - Faculty members from the Business Schools in the University of California system

- **Where will it be held?**
  - Marriott Hotel, San Francisco
  - Crown Room

- **Dates and times?**
  - February 14, 15
  - 9 a.m.–5 p.m. each day
  - Complete agenda available week before conference

- **What if I can't attend?**
  - Ask Josie at ext. 405 for presentation reports

- **How and where do I sign up?**
  - Josie has all the forms—due January 31

- **Who is responsible for travel and housing arrangements?**
  - Sue at Whole Universe Travel

- **Who is paying the airfare and hotel expenses?**
  - The company

Joan groups the points into categories. Then she writes a summary sentence for each category and puts them in order.

- **Logistics:** The conference is scheduled for February 14 and 15.

- **Topics:** Representatives from various organizations will make presentations on the newest performance evaluation strategies.

- **Speakers:** Speakers include experts in the field from business and academic organizations in the United States and abroad.

- **Arrangements:** The company is paying all expenses. Here's how to make arrangements and receive presentation reports if you cannot attend.

COMPLETED E-MAIL

To: Department Members
From: Joan Huang, Department Manager
Subject: Annual conference

Here is the information you've been waiting for about the upcoming conference, "Newest Trends in Evaluating Performance."

Logistics

The conference is scheduled for February 14 and 15. All events will take place in the Crown Room of the San Francisco Marriott Hotel between 9:00 a.m. and 5:00 p.m. A detailed agenda will be available the week of February 6.

Topics

Representatives from various organizations will make presentations on the newest performance evaluation strategies, including the following:

- The newest computer-based appraisal systems now being tested in the U.S., U.K., and Japan

- Case studies that explore the advantages and pitfalls of using 360° feedback

- Methods of preparing employees to conduct successful peer evaluations

Speakers

Speakers include experts in the field from business organizations and academic institutions in the United States and abroad. We expect representatives from the National Institute of Performance, the National Human Resources Organization, leading European organizations, and the Business Schools of the University of California system.

Arrangements

The company is paying all expenses. Here's how to make arrangements or receive the presentation reports if you cannot attend:

- To sign up, call Josie at extension 405 for a registration form. Make sure to return the form to Josie by 5:00 p.m. on January 31.

- To make air and hotel reservations, call Sue at Whole Universe Travel at (510) 655-6477.

- If you cannot attend, ask Josie to put your name on the distribution list for presentation reports.

If you have any questions about this conference, call me at extension 263. I hope you are able to attend.

REVIEW

You've reached the end of Lesson 1. Before applying what you've learned to a writing situation of your own, answer these review questions.

Write the correct word in the blanks. If you're not sure what to write or want to check your answer, turn to the page in parentheses to the right of the sentence.

1. To begin a writing plan, think about what you're going to write from your

    _____ point of view.   (15)

2. Decide on your primary purpose: to _____ or to

    _____ readers .   (18)

3. Compose a _____ that expresses your most

    important _____ .   (25)

4. To decide what information to include when you write, list the

    _____ and _____ that

    will accomplish your primary purpose.   (34)

5. If you're writing to influence readers, ask "_____

    should readers do what I want them to do?"   (34)

6. If you're writing to inform readers, ask "_____

    do readers need to know?"   (34)

7. After listing the facts and ideas to include in your writing, the next step is to

    _____ points into categories.   (38)

8. A _____ expands a category into a

    statement that introduces the paragraph's central topic, and tells readers why the topic is

    important.   (43)

Now you know how the planning process works. Before starting the next lesson, try the entire process with a writing situation of your own.

You have two options:

1. Complete Steps 4, 5, and 6 on the Writing Worksheet you already started working on.

    —OR—

2. Remove a new Worksheet from the back of this book and complete Steps 1–6 for a new writing situation.

When you have finished the writing plan, you may

- ■ Set it aside and move on to Lesson 2, where you'll learn to use the plan to write a first draft.

    —OR—

- ■ Do a quick first draft before beginning Lesson 2 and choose another situation for the assignment at the end of Lesson 2.

WHAT'S NEXT?

In Lesson 2 you will learn to use your writing plan to write a first draft. You'll see that once you have completed the six planning steps, you've already done most of the work. Only the final shaping is left.

2 WRITE THE FIRST DRAFT

INTRODUCTION

When you have completed your writing plan, the first draft almost writes itself. You've already done the hard work—deciding what you want to accomplish, finding the right words to express your main points, and selecting and organizing the facts and ideas you need to influence or inform readers.

The next step is to use that plan to write a first draft.

OBJECTIVES

In this lesson, you'll learn to write a professional and effective first draft by:

- Reviewing your writing plan and revising it as needed to make sure it is sound
- Writing an opening that catches readers' attention and clearly states what you are writing about
- Using transitions to link points, paragraphs, and sections smoothly
- Using lists to present information so readers can grasp it quickly
- Writing a closing that sums up points as needed and tells readers clearly what happens next

WHAT YOU NEED

- Two or three samples of your writing
- The writing plan that you completed in Lesson 1

REVIEW YOUR WRITING PLAN

Before starting the first draft, take a few moments to review your writing plan. There are two reasons for doing this:

- If there are any inconsistencies in the plan, it's important to correct them before you begin the first draft.
- This review helps you keep your plan in mind when you start writing—particularly if time has passed since you finished planning.

Here are some questions to ask as you review your writing plan:

- Have I considered my readers' point of view?

- Have I correctly identified my primary purpose?

- Does my key sentence accomplish my primary purpose?

  WRITING TO INFLUENCE

    Explain why readers should do what I want them to do?

  WRITING TO INFORM

    Introduce and/or summarize what readers need to know?

- Have I eliminated unnecessary information?

- Have I included all necessary information?

- Have I organized the information logically and effectively—from the reader's point of view?

If you answer "No" to any of these questions, take a closer look at your writing plan. Before you start the first draft, be sure the plan accurately expresses what you intend to say.

WRITE AN INVITING OPENING

Why do you think that openings are important? Write down a few reasons here:

1. _____

2. _____

3. _____

The first few lines of any piece of writing are extremely important. It is in the opening paragraph that you must catch your readers' attention, set the right tone, and make it clear what you are writing about.

Read these two openings. Which opening makes you want to continue?

E-MAIL 1   This is in reference to your recent e-mail which was passed to this department for review. Unfortunately, the information you requested is not available at this point in time . . . .

E-MAIL 2   Thank you for asking about the August 5 computer class. I am sorry that we do not yet know the instructor's name or the location, but we should be able to send you all the details by July 15.

You probably preferred the opening of E-Mail 2. E-Mail 1's opening uses a lot of clichés such as, "This is in reference to . . . ." It communicates little specific information.

The opening of E-Mail 1, in contrast, was clearly written by one person to another. It responds directly to specific questions. The writer gets to the point quickly and provides details.

Here are the criteria for an effective opening:

- It establishes a personal contact with the reader and sets the right tone—particularly important tasks when your primary purpose is to influence
- It catches the reader's attention
- It includes a key sentence that tells the reader what you are writing about
- It is no more than three or four sentences long

Here are some examples of openings. In each set, put an **X** next to the opening you think best meets the criteria.

_____ A) We hereby acknowledge receiving your message dated April 20. Your complaint has been taken under advisement.

_____ B) Thank you for telling us about the missing parts in the equipment you recently purchased. We will be happy to replace the parts, but we need the following information . . . .

_____ A) Per your recent inquiry concerning delivery of your car, a fax was sent to the attention of the manufacturer. We are pleased to provide you with a photocopy of the response we received.

_____ B) We are happy to say that your car will arrive in port on Wednesday, August 1. You can pick it up any time after noon on Thursday, August 2.

If you preferred Opening B in each set, then you recognize an effective opening.

One quick way to improve openings is to avoid overused phrases like these:

With reference to …	Regarding your recent communication …
Pursuant to …	We are in receipt of your message …
Enclosed, please find …	On the above date and time …
Please be advised …	This is in regards to …
Attached herewith …	Per your request …
I am writing to inform you …	

Here are some examples of how to replace overused phrases with simple, direct language:

OVERUSED	SIMPLE AND DIRECT
Per your request for shipping instructions . . .	As you asked, here are the instructions for preparing your shipment.
Please be advised that your shipment has been delayed.	Unfortunately, your shipment has been delayed.
Enclosed, please find copies of your last three invoices.	I have enclosed copies of your last three invoices. I am sending copies of your last three invoices. Here are copies of your last three invoices.
I am writing to inform you that your shipment has been located.	We have found your shipment.
This is in regards to your recent communication regarding our service.	Thank you for telling us that you appreciated our customer service team's quick response to your questions about our software.
We are in receipt of your message in regards to the vacant position.	As you asked, we are happy to send you an application for the position of Community Relations Director.

EXERCISE

Using your imagination to fill in missing details, revise the following openings so they cover the following points:

- make a personal contact with the reader, set the right tone, and catch the reader's attention

- include a key sentence that tells the reader what you are writing about

- are no more than three or four sentences long

Hint It will be easier to revise the openings if you look at the message from the reader's point of view.

OPENING 1

Please be advised that your comments on the proposed Computer Training Program, received by this office on June 3, have been reviewed and, where appropriate, incorporated into the program.

_____

_____

_____

_____

_____

_____

OPENING 2

I am writing to inform you that payment has not yet been received for the current month. The conditions of your note specify that payment be made no later than the first day of each month. It is imperative that payment be received within 10 days of the date of this message.

_____

_____

_____

_____

_____

_____

OPENING 3

Attached please find a copy of the Assistant Director's message to
Acme Products. Also attached is a copy of the message to Alex Stein
from Acme's CEO, as well as a copy of the Test Plan form, which was
written by Bill Jordan.

_____

_____

_____

ANSWERS

Here are the kinds of changes you might have made.

OPENING 1

ORIGINAL   Please be advised that your comments on the proposed Computer Training
Program, received by this office on June 3, have been reviewed and, where appropriate, incorporated into the program.

REVISION   Thank you for your comments on the proposed Computer Training Program.
We have incorporated the suggested changes listed below.

OPENING 2

ORIGINAL   I am writing to inform you that payment has not yet been received for the current
month. The conditions of your loan specify that payment be made no later than
the first day of each month. It is imperative that payment be received within 10
days of the date of this message.

REVISION   We have not yet received the loan payment that was due on April 1. Please make
sure we receive it no later than April 25.

OPENING 3

ORIGINAL   Attached please find a copy of the Assistant Director's message to Acme Products.
Also attached is a copy of the message to Alex Stein from Acme's CEO, as well as a
copy of the Test Plan form, which was written by Bill Jordan.

REVISION   I'm enclosing copies of the following:
- the Assistant Director's message to Acme Products
- the Acme CEO's message to Alex Stein
- Bill Jordan's Test Plan form

SUMMARIES

When you're writing a report, business plan, or proposal, consider including a **summary** for your reader. Summaries, also known as *report summaries* and *executive summaries*, serve a different purpose from introductions or background statements.

Under most circumstances, an **introduction** or **background statement** is read by people who will read the rest of the document. The purpose is to establish a context for what people are going to read.

On the other hand, a summary might be read by people who will never see—or never read—the entire document. Summaries are designed for people who need to know your most important message and the key facts you have included to inform or influence your reader about that important message.

It's a good idea to write the summary after you've developed the writing plan. Then you can use the summary statements from the writing plan to develop your report or executive summary.

Keep the following points in mind when you write summaries:

- Always state your most important message at the beginning of the summary

- Put the summary at the beginning of the document

- Keep the summary short (between half a page and a full page is ideal; some experts say that a summary should be no longer than one tenth of the entire document)

- Make sure that the summary covers all the main points and that they are in the same order as in the main document

- Focus on the most important points—remember that readers can turn to the main document if they want or need more details

TRANSITIONS

To make your writing more readable, use transitions to connect your ideas. A transition is a word, phrase, or sentence that relates a new topic to the previous one, smoothly connecting the parts of a piece of writing.

Transitions are rather like the cartilage and tendons that hold your bones together. They form a connective tissue that links your ideas to one another. In writing, transitions show readers how your ideas fit together, help you achieve continuity, and help readers follow your points easily.

Read this e-mail. Notice how the boldfaced words and phrases serve as transitions, helping the reader see the connection between points.

> Alex:
>
> Thanks for calling yesterday to ask about this year's sales conference. The Planning Committee is running a little behind schedule, **but** I'm happy to tell you what we know so far.
>
> Despite the problem we had with meeting space last year, we've decided to give Lazy Acres another try. Everyone rates the other facilities very highly. **In particular,** people like the tennis courts and exercise equipment. **Also,** the guest rooms are spacious, so we can use them for small group meetings.
>
> Although the date is still under discussion, we're looking at the second week in August. We are, **however,** also considering September; **for one thing,** the August date might interfere with people's vacation plans.
>
> **Unless** we run into a snag, we hope to have firm plans by the end of the month. I'll let you know what I know as soon as I know it. **Until then**, feel free to pass this information on to your staff.

Here are examples of words and phrases you can use to link points, sections and paragraphs:

ADDITIONS
again
also
and also
as well as
as you asked
equally important
for one thing
further
furthermore
in addition
moreover
next
now

CONTRASTS
although
but
despite
however
nevertheless
unless
until

RESULT
accordingly
as a consequence
as a result
consequently
for that reason
thus

COMPARISONS
equally
in the same way
similarly

EMPHASIS
above all
certainly
especially
indeed
in fact
in other words
in particular
of course

SUMMARY
finally
on the whole
to sum up

PRACTICE

Underline the transitions in this message. Notice how they help link the points and improve the tone.

Dear Frieda:

As you asked, I am happy to suggest a marketing consultant for your new project. The person I recommend most highly is Kate Jackson.

I worked with Kate for two years at Vision West. Although we were in different departments, we worked together on at least five projects. She was reliable and pleasant. Best of all, she seemed to have a never-ending store of creative ideas, although she never tried to impose them on the group. In fact, she was quite willing to drop any plan that didn't seem workable.

Unless Kate's situation has changed since I last spoke to her in May, I suspect she will be very interested in your position. She will, of course, want to know something about the opportunities it offers for advancement.

I hope Kate works out for you. If not, give me a call and I'll keep my eyes open for someone else.

Did you underline these transitions?

> Dear Frieda:
>
> As you asked, I am happy to suggest a marketing consultant for your new project. The person I recommend most highly is Kate Jackson.
>
> I worked with Kate for two years at Vision West. <u>Although</u> we were in different departments, we worked together on at least five projects. She was reliable and pleasant. <u>Best of all</u>, she seemed to have a never-ending store of creative ideas, <u>although</u> she never tried to impose them on the group. <u>In fact</u>, she was quite willing to drop any plan that didn't seem workable.
>
> <u>Unless</u> Kate's situation has changed since I last spoke to her in May, I suspect she will be very interested in your position. She will, <u>of course</u>, want to know something about the opportunities it offers for advancement.
>
> I hope Kate works out for you. <u>If not</u>, give me a call and I'll keep my eyes open for someone else.

USING LISTS

How do you read business documents? Chances are, you don't linger over the words the way you'd linger over a novel. Instead, you probably scan the document to pick out the main points and the details you need.

Taking the reader's point of view, it's easy to see that paragraphs are not always the best way to present information. The more technical or complicated the information, the more likely it is to be lost when it's presented in paragraph form.

Your goal as a writer is to help readers find information as quickly as possible. To show consideration and speed things up for your reader, look for opportunities to present information in lists.

Read the examples on the next two pages. They both present the same information, but look how much easier this information is to scan when it's in list form.

ORIGINAL

Dear Ms. Fratelli:

To process your loan application, we need the following information and documents as soon as possible.

In item 12A, please enter the name and address of the lender who holds your second deed of trust. The current balances on all your credit cards and outstanding loans should be entered in items 16B and 16C, except for your automobile loans (item 16D).

The name and address of your previous employers should be entered in Item 6C if you have been at your current job for less than two years. Include an explanation of any gap in employment during the past ten years.

List the balances on your bank accounts in item 4A. Include the name and address of the institution and the account number. Use items 4B, C, and D for certificates of deposit, stocks, etc., as shown.

The purpose of the loan should be entered in item 3, along with the amount requested. Finally, be sure to sign and date the form in item 23. The completed form should be sent to the loan processor along with copies of your last two years' tax returns and copies of your most recent pay stubs.

Please let me know if you have questions.

Sincerely,

REVISION

Dear Ms. Fratelli:

To process your loan, we need a completed application as soon as possible. Please send the completed form to the loan processor along with copies of the following two documents:

- Your last two years' tax returns

- Your most recent pay stubs

On the application form, please complete the following items:

- Describe the purpose of the loan and enter the amount requested.

- List the balances on your bank accounts (4A). Enter the name and address of the institution and the account number. List any certificates of deposit, stocks, etc., as shown (4B, 4C, and 4D).

- If you have been at your current job for less than two years, enter the name and address of your previous employers (6C). Include an explanation of any gap in employment during the past ten years.

- Enter the name and address of the lender who holds your second deed of trust (12A).

- List the current balances on all your credit cards (16B), outstanding loans (16C), and automobile loans (16D).

- Sign and date the form (Item 23).

Please let me know if you have questions.

Sincerely,

GUIDELINES FOR USING LISTS

You can use a list in business writing—and, often, you should use a list—whenever you present three or more related pieces of information. Lists are more effective than long paragraphs because they

- communicate information quickly

- save valuable writing time

- reduce the chance of grammar and punctuation errors

To make sure your lists are easy to read, follow the five guidelines below. Full illustrations of each of these guidelines follow the list.

1. **Introduce the list.** Every list needs an introductory statement, if only a few words, that tells readers what the list is about and puts the list items in context. Make sure that you leave a space between the introductory statement and the first list item.

2. **Make sure that all items belong on the list.** All items on the list should relate directly to the introductory statement.

3. **Be consistent with initial capitalization, sentence structure, and end punctuation.**

   - If you capitalize the first word of one line, capitalize the first word in every line.

   - Items in any single list should all be complete sentences, or all be sentence fragments. List items that are sentence fragments should not end in periods, and do not have to begin with capital letters (unless the first word is a proper noun).

   - For lists of complete sentences, end punctuation (periods or question marks) is only necessary for each item if any item contains more than one sentence. In any list of complete sentences, you must use end punctuation after *all* the list's items if even *one* list item has end punctuation.

4. **Keep the list parallel in form.** For example, if one item begins with an *-ing* verb tense, then all items should begin with *-ing* verbs.

5. **Organize the list for your readers.** Lists that include more than five or six items can be difficult to follow. Make lists easier to read by organizing the items into main points and subpoints.

Here are examples to illustrate the five guidelines for lists that you just read.

1. **Introduce the list.**

    A list should never stand alone: it needs an introductory statement. The first item in a list can't introduce the list itself.

    WITHOUT AN INTRODUCTION

    - We offer several thank-you gifts

    - A 10% discount on purchases during May

    - A discount coupon for the Milano Ristorante

    - A complimentary bottle of our best olive oil

    WITH AN INTRODUCTION

    To express our appreciation for your business, we would like to offer you a choice of the following thank-you gifts:

    - A 10% discount on purchases during May

    - A discount coupon for the Milano Ristorante

    - A complimentary bottle of our best olive oil

2. **Make sure that all items belong on the list.** All items on the list should relate directly to the introductory statement.

    NOT ALL ITEMS RELATE TO THE INTRODUCTORY STATEMENT

    To prepare the room for training, please do the following:

    - Set up the tables in a **U** shape

    - Put two flipcharts in the front of the classroom

    - Place the projector on the table in the corner

    - Make sure that there are lots of exercises and opportunities to practice

ALL ITEMS RELATE TO THE INTRODUCTORY STATEMENT

When training is over, please do the following things:

- Recycle used flipchart pages

- Turn off the projector and store it in the closet

- Put the tables and chairs back the way you found them

- Give the completed evaluations to Melissa

3. **Be consistent with initial capitalization, sentences or sentence fragments, and end punctuation.**

Use end punctuation only when at least one item contains more than one complete sentence. In paragraphs, sentences' end punctuation (periods and question marks) tells readers when one sentence stops and another starts. In lists, end punctuation is only necessary if an item contains more than one sentence. That's because the format of a list clearly shows where one item stops and another begins. It's not wrong to use end punctuation for single sentences in a list. But if you use end punctuation for *one* item, you must use it for *all* items.

END PUNCTUATION UNNECESSARY

We are unable to meet the original deadline for the following reasons:

- Two team members resigned in October and we have been unable to replace them

- The client expanded the project scope

- Three weeks of heavy rain made it impossible to complete our investigation

END PUNCTUATION NECESSARY

Here is a summary of our findings:

- The costs of moving to a new location will be higher than we originally estimated.

- According to the most current figures, the total cost will exceed $150,000.

- If we delay the move for five years, we will need an additional 10,000 square feet of space.

- Only 30 percent of our employees say they would be willing to move out of California. Over 60 percent, however, would be willing to consider a move within the northern area of the state.

The following list is hard to read because its format is inconsistent.

INCONSISTENT

We are unable to meet the original deadline for the following reasons:

- Two team members resigned in October. We have been unable to re-place them.

- expanded project scope

- Three weeks of heavy rain made it impossible to complete our investigation

The periods in the first item are inconsistent with the complete sentence in the third item, which has no period. The uncapitalized sentence fragment is distracting because its form is inconsistent with the other two items. As a general rule, start bulleted items with a capital; it looks more professional.

Here's the same list in a consistent format.

CONSISTENT

We are unable to meet the original deadline for the following reasons:

- Two team members resigned in October and we have been unable to replace them

- The client expanded the project scope

- Three weeks of heavy rain made it impossible to complete our investigation

4. **Keep the list parallel in form.**

The items in a list must be parallel—presented in the same forms. For example, if one item begins with a verb, all the items must begin with verbs. If one item is a complete sentence, all the items must be complete sentences.

NOT PARALLEL

The agenda for the March meeting includes the following:

- Discussion of the new health plan, which will be available to all permanent full-time employees

- Whether to revise the procedures manual

- Early-retirement policy

PARALLEL

At the March meeting, we will do the following:

- Discuss the new health plan, which will be available to all permanent full-time employees

- Decide whether to revise the procedures manual

- Draft an early-retirement policy

> For more about parallel structure, see Lesson 5: Use Correct Grammar, page 137.

5. **Organize the list for your reader.**

As a general rule, keep lists short. There should be no more than five or six items on your list. When long lists are necessary, reorganize them as two or more shorter lists. Make long lists easier for your readers to scan by organizing the items into main points and subpoints.

TOO MANY ITEMS

Please supply the following for the conference that begins on October 22:

- 30 writing tablets for each meeting room

- Five laptops for the community room

- An overhead projector for each meeting room

- Coffee, tea, and pastry in the foyer each morning

- Four round tables for each meeting room

- At least five telephones with outside lines in the community room

- A basket of fruit for each table in the meeting rooms

- A registration table in the foyer

ITEMS ORGANIZED WITH SUBPOINTS

Please supply the following for the conference that begins on October 22:

In each meeting room:

- 30 writing tablets

- An overhead projector

- Four round tables

- A basket of fruit for each table

In the community room:

- Five laptops

- At least five telephones with outside lines

In the foyer:

- Coffee, tea, and pastry each morning

- A registration table

TRY IT
. . . .

Use the space below or a blank sheet of paper to rewrite this paragraph in list format. Remember to include an introductory statement that tells readers what the list is about and establishes the context. Remember to follow the guidelines on page 73.

> The task force found that the customer service representatives need training in how to respond to problems and complaints. There is widespread unhappiness about the quality of food in the cafeteria, indicating the need to find another vendor. How to implement flexible hours without creating logistical problems requires additional study. Finally, field representatives need more powerful laptops, which have not been included in this year's budget. These are the primary areas of concern the members of the task force believe they need to address during the next six months.

_____

_____

_____

_____

_____

_____

_____

_____

_____

_____

_____

_____

_____

_____

_____

_____

_____

Here are two ways to revise that paragraph into a list:

REVISION 1

Below are the primary areas of concern the members of the task force believe they need to address during the next six months:

- The customer service representatives need training in how to respond to problems and complaints

- There is widespread unhappiness about the quality of food in the cafeteria, indicating the need to find another vendor

- Additional study is needed to determine how to implement flexible hours without creating logistical problems

- Field representatives need more powerful laptops, which have not been included in this year's budget

REVISION 2

The task force members believe they must do the following during the next six months:

- Train customer service representatives to respond to problems and complaints

- Search for a new vendor who will improve the quality of food in the cafeteria

- Study ways to implement flexible hours without creating logistical problems

- Find funds to provide field representatives with the more powerful laptops they need

TRY IT   Use the space below or a blank sheet of paper to rewrite and reformat this paragraph
....   as a list.

> To help us update our database, please review the enclosed
> listings and notify us of any changes. First, proofread each
> listing and indicate any necessary corrections. Then please
> enter the best address for clients to reach you and at the
> same time verify that the telephone and fax numbers and e-
> mail addresses are correct. Finally, if you wish, you may add
> a maximum of two lines of explanation to each listing.

REVISION

Here's one way to present the information more effectively. Your version might differ.

> To help us update our database, please review the enclosed listings and notify us of any changes:
>
> - Proofread each listing and indicate any necessary corrections
>
> - Enter the best address for clients to reach you
>
> - Verify that telephone and fax numbers and e-mail addresses are correct
>
> - If you wish, add a maximum of two lines of explanation to each listing

USING HEADINGS

Can you think of any reasons to use headings in your documents?

1. _____

2. _____

The Benefits of Headings

- Headings make it easier for people to find information. At work, people don't read every word of every document.

- Headings make a document more attractive by creating an organized visual layout. Research shows that long, dense paragraphs are the most difficult and discouraging way to present information to your readers. Headings are a good way to break up dense text.

- Headings force you to group relevant facts and information together. This makes your document easier for readers to follow.

Headings make your documents easier to understand by presenting your reader with concise themes. Headings are essential if your document is long or complicated, or contains technical information. The planning process itself helps you come up with the headings: once you group information into categories, the headings practically identify themselves.

Here's a single e-mail without headings, and then with them.

WITHOUT HEADINGS

> Ali:
>
> Hope you can come to the meeting this summer. The annual presidents' circle sales meeting will be held at the Hilton in San Francisco and you should bring your updated presentations and spreadsheets. You can make travel arrangements yourself or Pam can help you. We'll have one day of learning with workshop leaders including Jamie Hartwell, Linda Lou, and Peter Panino, and one day to look internally at our processes with Jack Deiner.
>
> We're going to Alcatraz. It will be three days long with an optional dinner on Tuesday night. Sally is no longer available to help with travel arrangements. Another agenda will be sent out. You can come on Wednesday morning or Tuesday night but make sure that you're there till Friday morning. Bring comfortable walking shoes. If you make the travel arrangements yourself, use billing code 55789. You don't need

to bring anything else. You were selected because you did a great job.

WITH HEADINGS

Subject: Annual Presidents' Circle Sales Meeting, July 14–17, 2009

Ali:

Because of the great job you did this year, you've been invited to the Presidents' Circle Sales Meeting in San Francisco this summer. Following is all the information you'll need to make your travel arrangements. We'll send you a more detailed agenda by May 1.

Meeting Dates and Location

The meeting will be held in the San Francisco Hilton from Tuesday, July 14th, through Friday, July 17th, 2009.

Travel Arrangements

The travel process has changed; Sally is no longer available to help. You can make arrangements yourself using your company credit card and billing code 55789, or ask Pam to help.

What to Bring

Please bring your updated spreadsheets and presentations. Also, bring comfortable walking shoes for an outing to Alcatraz on Friday morning. We'll provide everything else you need.

Agenda

- Tuesday: meet for dinner at the hotel restaurant at 7 p.m. (optional)

- Wednesday: meetings 9–5 with Jamie Hartwell, Linda Lou, and Peter Panino, followed by dinner at Aziza

- Thursday: meetings 9–5 with Jack Deiner followed by dinner at La Mar Cebicheria

- Friday: morning excursion to Alcatraz; meeting convenes at 1 p.m.

That's it! Please let me know if you have any questions. I'll send out a detailed agenda by May 1st. Thanks, and congratulations!

CLOSING PARAGRAPHS

A strong closing achieves the following goals:

- makes a final personal contact with readers (a crucial factor when you're writing to influence)
- wraps up any loose ends
- tells readers clearly what happens next
- uses specific language

A closing paragraph might also do the following:

- restate what readers should do
- restate what readers should know

Compare these two closings. Which do you prefer?

CLOSING 1   It would be appreciated if this situation could be rectified in a timely manner. Any questions can be addressed to this writer at the above address.

CLOSING 2   Please find the missing file by June 15. If I can help in any way, please call me at (510) 655-6477.

You probably preferred Closing 2. The first closing is impersonal and vague. The second is specific to the situation and conveys useful information.

Here are examples of the kinds of clichés that sound tired—as if they were produced by a machine rather than by a person.

Please contact the undersigned regarding time constraints on this policy.

Your assistance and cooperation will be greatly appreciated.

Do not hesitate to contact this writer should you require additional information.

Minor changes can transform those closings by making them specific to the piece of writing.

INSTEAD OF ...	**TRY THIS ...**
Please contact the above regarding time constraints on this policy.	Please call John Alcotts about the expiration date on this policy.
Your assistance and cooperation will be greatly appreciated.	I will be grateful for any help you can give me in tracking down the correct phone number.
Do not hesitate to contact this writer should you require additional information.	If you need a map or specific directions, please let me know.

PRACTICE

Write a closing for this message.

> Dear Mr. Hogan:
>
> Thank you for asking about our new Flexible Loan Program. I'm happy to send a brochure that describes the program and includes an application.
>
> We designed this program after many discussions with customers about what types of lending arrangements they wanted. I think you'll find it offers some unique ways of meeting your financial needs.

_____

_____

_____

_____

_____

_____

_____

Turn the page to see an example of a closing you might have written.

ANSWER

Here's one possible conclusion for the message.

Dear Mr. Hogan:

Thank you for asking about our new Flexible Loan Program. I'm happy to send a brochure that describes the program and includes an application.

We designed this program after many discussions with customers about what types of lending arrangements they wanted. I think you'll find it offers some unique ways of meeting your financial needs.

Please let me know if you have questions about this loan program. If I haven't heard from you, I'll call in two weeks to see if you'd like to apply for a loan under this new program.

REVIEW

Fill in the blanks with the correct word or phrase. If you're not sure what to write, turn to the page number in the parentheses to the right of the sentence.

1. Before starting to write the first draft, always

    _____ your writing plan.   (59)

2. An effective opening:

    ■ establishes a _____ contact with the_____

    ■ catches the reader's _____

    ■ includes a key sentence that tells the reader what you are _____

       _____

    ■ is no more than _____ or

    ■ _____ sentences long   (61)

3. Use transitions to _____ your ideas.   (67)

4. A strong closing:

    ■ makes a final _____

    ■ _____ with readers

    ■ may _____ the main point

    ■ wraps up any _____

    ■ tells readers clearly what _____

    ■ uses _____ language   (85)

Now turn the page for an assignment.

It's time to try out everything you've learned in this lesson.

You will draft a document, using the writing plan you completed at the end of Lesson 1.

OPTION: If you wish, you may start with a new situation. But be sure to use a new Writing Worksheet to develop a new writing plan. Don't ignore everything you've learned so far by starting a draft without a plan!

WRITING WORKSHEET

SUBJECT:

1. LOOK AT WHAT YOU'RE GOING TO WRITE FROM YOUR READERS' POINT OF VIEW.

    Name or describe reader(s): _____

    Think about your readers' needs, interests, and concerns. Then check the appropriate boxes:

    IS YOUR READER ...
    - expecting to hear from you?
    - familiar with the subject?
    - already interested in what you have to say?
    - likely to consider you an authority on the subject?
    - likely to find what you have to say useful?
    - familiar with your views on the subject?
    - already committed to a point of view?
    - likely to agree with your point of view?
    - likely to find your message uncomfortable?
    - (other needs, interests, and concerns)

2. DECIDE ON YOUR PRIMARY PURPOSE:

    ☐ INFLUENCE   ☐ INFORM

3. COMPOSE A KEY SENTENCE THAT EXPRESSES YOUR MOST IMPORTANT MESSAGE:

    I want my reader(s) to do or to know:

    _____

    _____

    _____

    _____

    _____

4. LIST THE FACTS AND IDEAS TO INCLUDE:

_____

_____

_____

_____

_____

_____

_____

_____

_____

_____

_____

_____

_____

_____

_____

_____

_____

_____

_____

_____

_____

_____

_____

Continue on another page if necessary.

5. GROUP POINTS INTO CATEGORIES (Key points):

_____

_____

_____

_____

_____

_____

_____

_____

_____

6. WRITE A SUMMARY STATEMENT OF ONE TO THREE SENTENCES FOR EACH CATEGORY, AND PUT THEM IN ORDER.

_____

_____

_____

_____

_____

_____

_____

_____

Continue on another page if necessary.

WRITING WORKSHEET

SUBJECT:

1. LOOK AT WHAT YOU'RE GOING TO WRITE FROM YOUR READERS' POINT OF VIEW.

   Name or describe reader(s): _____

   Think about your readers' needs, interests, and concerns. Then check the appropriate boxes:

   IS YOUR READER ...

   - expecting to hear from you?
   - familiar with the subject?
   - already interested in what you have to say?
   - likely to consider you an authority on the subject?
   - likely to find what you have to say useful?
   - familiar with your views on the subject?
   - already committed to a point of view?
   - likely to agree with your point of view?
   - likely to find your message uncomfortable?
   - (other needs, interests, and concerns)

2. DECIDE ON YOUR PRIMARY PURPOSE:

   ☐ INFLUENCE   ☐ INFORM

3. COMPOSE A KEY SENTENCE THAT EXPRESSES YOUR MOST IMPORTANT MESSAGE:

   I want my reader(s) to do or to know:

   _____

   _____

   _____

   _____

   _____

4. LIST THE FACTS AND IDEAS TO INCLUDE:

_____

_____

_____

_____

_____

_____

_____

_____

_____

_____

_____

_____

_____

_____

_____

_____

_____

_____

_____

_____

_____

_____

_____

_____

_____

_____

Continue on another page if necessary.

5. GROUP POINTS INTO CATEGORIES (Key points):

_____

_____

_____

_____

_____

_____

_____

_____

_____

_____

6. WRITE A SUMMARY STATEMENT OF ONE TO THREE SENTENCES FOR EACH CATEGORY, AND PUT THEM IN ORDER.

_____

_____

_____

_____

_____

_____

_____

_____

_____

Continue on another page if necessary.

WRITING WORKSHEET

SUBJECT:

1. LOOK AT WHAT YOU'RE GOING TO WRITE FROM YOUR READERS' POINT OF VIEW.

   Name or describe reader(s): _____

   Think about your readers' needs, interests, and concerns. Then check the appropriate boxes:

   IS YOUR READER …

   - expecting to hear from you?
   - familiar with the subject?
   - already interested in what you have to say?
   - likely to consider you an authority on the subject?
   - likely to find what you have to say useful?
   - familiar with your views on the subject?
   - already committed to a point of view?
   - likely to agree with your point of view?
   - likely to find your message uncomfortable?
   - (other needs, interests, and concerns)

2. DECIDE ON YOUR PRIMARY PURPOSE:

   ☐ INFLUENCE   ☐ INFORM

3. COMPOSE A KEY SENTENCE THAT EXPRESSES YOUR MOST IMPORTANT MESSAGE:

   I want my reader(s) to do or to know:

   _____

   _____

   _____

   _____

   _____

4. LIST THE FACTS AND IDEAS TO INCLUDE:

_____

_____

_____

_____

_____

_____

_____

_____

_____

_____

_____

_____

_____

_____

_____

_____

_____

_____

_____

_____

_____

_____

Continue on another page if necessary.

5. GROUP POINTS INTO CATEGORIES (Key points):

_____

_____

_____

_____

_____

_____

_____

_____

_____

6. WRITE A SUMMARY STATEMENT OF ONE TO THREE SENTENCES FOR EACH CATEGORY, AND PUT THEM IN ORDER.

_____

_____

_____

_____

_____

_____

_____

_____

Continue on another page if necessary.

WHAT'S NEXT?

The next four lessons give you tools to shape the final language of your document. In Lesson 3, you will learn how to use concise language.

3   USE CONCISE LANGUAGE

INTRODUCTION

Unnecessary words are obstacles to good business writing. They clutter up your sentences and slow your readers down. They can also make your documents boring. By eliminating unnecessary words, you can keep your readers' interest and make your writing easier to follow.

OBJECTIVES

In this lesson, you'll learn to write more professionally and effectively with these strategies:

- Finding single words for one-word ideas

- Avoiding repetition

- Eliminating wasteful verbs and clauses

WHAT YOU NEED

- The draft document that you completed in Lesson 1

- Samples of your writing

Here are a few examples of sentence with clutter—words that take up space without adding meaning. Which words do you think are unnecessary? Can you eliminate any words?

- Please let me know as to whether you will attend the party.

- The noise level of the trains arriving and departing from the station is low by the current standards of the rapid-transit industry.

- There are several employees who want to take vacations in June.

Here are the words you could easily eliminate:

- Please let me know ~~as to~~ whether you will attend the party.

- The noise level of the ~~trains~~ arriving and departing ∧ _trains_ ~~from the station~~ is low by ~~the~~ current standards ∧⊙ ~~of the rapid-transit industry.~~

- ~~There are several~~ ∧ _Several_ employees ~~who~~ want to take vacations in June.

In this lesson, you'll look at several ways to get rid of unnecessary words and you'll practice revising wordy sentences. Then you'll review your own writing to see if you can make it more concise.

USE ONE WORD FOR A ONE-WORD IDEA

Sometimes you can collapse several words or a long phrase into one word that conveys your message quickly and clearly: for instance, *at a time prior to* simply means *before*. The longer phrase is dull and bulky. The single word does the same job more efficiently.

At other times, you can collapse a multiword phrase into one word by identifying the most important word of the phrase, turning that word into a different part of speech, and cutting out words that don't enhance your meaning.

ORIGINAL We **are in agreement** with you about the contract terms.

REVISION We <u>agree</u> with you about the contract terms.

ORIGINAL She solved the problem **in a clever way**.

REVISION She solved the problem <u>cleverly</u>.

      —OR—

    She <u>cleverly</u> solved the problem.

In the first example, the short verb "agree" delivers the full meaning of the longer phrase "are in agreement."

In the second example, "clever" is the most important word in the phrase "in a clever way." The single word "cleverly" delivers the same meaning faster.

Try a practice exercise on the next page.

PRACTICE

Eliminate unnecessary words or revise the sentences to make them more concise.

ORIGINAL The client visited the site of the project in May.

REVISION The client visited <u>the project site</u> in May.

1. She drove in a reckless manner.

   _____

   _____

2. We conducted a survey of the members.

   _____

   _____

3. The manager made an offer to buy everyone coffee.

   _____

   _____

4. I believe this procedure will make an improvement in the way reports are filed.

   _____

   _____

5. He called us in regard to his recent insurance claim.

   _____

   _____

6. Due to the fact that she had been drinking, the accident was her fault.

   _____

   _____

Check your answers on the next page.

Your answers should look something like this:

1. She drove <u>recklessly</u>.

2. We <u>surveyed</u> the members.

3. The manager <u>offered</u> to buy everyone coffee.

4. I believe this procedure will <u>improve</u> how reports are filed.

5. He called us <u>about</u> his recent insurance claim.

6. <u>Because</u> she had been drinking, the accident was her fault.

AVOID REPETITION

Business writers often use two or more words that mean exactly the same thing, leading to unnecessarily wordy sentences. Here are some common repetitive phrases:

alternative choices	equally as effective as	separate entities
basic fundamentals	symptoms indicative of	advance warning
serious crisis	desirable benefits	two halves
final outcome	important essentials	regular weekly meetings
past experience	end result	absolutely complete
surrounding circumstances	future plans	ten a.m. in the morning

A crisis is always serious, plans are always for the future, and ten a.m. doesn't happen at night. These unnecessary words waste your readers' time.

PRACTICE

Eliminate the unnecessary repetitions in these sentences.

1. The urban residents of the city are unhappy with the new regulations.

   _____

   _____

2. The subterranean garage, located underground, is more secure than the old one.

   _____

   _____

3. Until last week, our group had the best record to date.

   _____

   _____

Your revisions should look something like this. The underlined words convey the original sentences' full meaning without the wasteful extra words on the last page.

1. The <u>urban</u> residents are unhappy with the new regulations.

    —OR—

    The <u>city</u> residents are unhappy with the new regulations.

2. The <u>subterranean</u> garage is more secure than the old one.

3. <u>Until last week</u>, our group had the best record.

ELIMINATE WASTEFUL POSSESSIVES, CLAUSES, AND *THERE IS* PHRASES

Some possessive word forms add nothing to a sentence but unnecessary length.

ORIGINAL **Their assumption is that** the company should always come first.

REVISION <u>They assume</u> the company should always come first.

Some sentences can be streamlined by removing unnecessary *who*, *that*, and *which* clauses.

ORIGINAL The broker **who works in Chicago** sent the file **that is incomplete** to the home office.

REVISION The <u>Chicago</u> broker sent the <u>incomplete</u> file to the home office.

Also, phrases such as *there is*, *there are*, and *there may be* can clutter up sentences—either on their own or by requiring extra words after the phrase.

ORIGINAL **There is** a new package on your desk.

REVISION A new package <u>is</u> on your desk.

ORIGINAL **There may be** several applicants **who** have the necessary background for this position.

REVISION Several applicants <u>may</u> have the necessary background for this position.

PRACTICE

Revise these sentences to make them more concise.

1. The members of the group who are interested in learning more about this software are welcome to attend the demonstration that will be conducted on February 16.

   _____

   _____

   _____

2. Tomorrow's meeting, which will be held as always on the fourth floor, will include a speech about literacy in the workplace.

   _____

   _____

   _____

3. There are thousands of hours wasted because no one can use the files that are out of date.

   _____

   _____

   _____

Your revisions should be similar to these:

- The group members interested in learning more about this software are welcome to attend the February 16 demonstration.

- Tomorrow's fourth-floor meeting will include a speech about literacy in the workplace.

- Thousands of hours are wasted because no one can use the out-of-date files.

PRACTICE

Here's a chance to pull together what you've learned so far. These sentences contain several kinds of clutter. Revise them to be more concise.

> On the basis of your recent letter, I would like to take this opportunity to inform you that I will investigate the problem about the delay in processing your loan that you mentioned and send you a letter in order to report my findings.
>
> At this point in time, it is our understanding that the new computer system will have the capability of processing 50 percent more information than the amount that is processed by our present system.
>
> With regard to the current status of your request for additional office equipment, we have submitted a request for the purpose of obtaining the funds that are needed to initiate the purchase.

_____

_____

_____

_____

_____

_____

_____

_____

_____

Check your answers on the next page.

Your revisions should look something like this:

~~On the basis of your recent letter,~~ I would like ~~to take this opportunity~~
to inform you that I will investigate ~~the problem about~~ the delay in

processing your loan ~~which you mentioned~~ and ~~send you a letter in~~
~~order to report~~ *write you with* ^ my findings.

—OR—

Thank you for
~~On the basis of~~ ^ your recent letter ^ ~~I would like to take this opportu-~~
~~nity to inform you that~~ I will investigate ~~the problem about~~ the delay in

processing your loan ~~which you mentioned,~~ and send you a letter ~~in~~
~~order to report~~ *with* ^ my findings.

We understand
~~At this point in time, it is our~~ ^ ~~understanding that~~ the new computer
be able to
system will ~~have the capability of~~ ^ processing 50 percent more infor-

mation ^ ~~than the amount which is processed by our present system.~~

—OR—

We now understand
~~At this point in time, it is our~~ ^ ~~understanding that~~ the new computer

system will ~~have the capability of~~ processing 50 percent more infor-

mation than ~~the amount which is processed by~~ our present system.

~~With regard to the current status of your request for additional office~~
We   requested
~~equipment, We~~ have ~~submitted a~~ ^ ~~request for the purpose of obtain-~~
to purchase the office equipment you requested.
~~ing the~~ funds ^ ~~that are needed to initiate the purchase.~~

You are probably getting good at spotting and eliminating clutter.
Turn the page for one last practice before searching your own writing
for unnecessary words.

PRACTICE

Revise these paragraphs to be as concise as possible without changing the meaning. You can cross out or write in words on this page without recopying the letter.

During the month of March, the people who are working on the HUF project team made a study of the past history of HUF in order to come to some conclusions as to whether the necessary information was available for the purpose of their determining the project goals.

The people who were members of this study team are of the opinion that the original analysis was done in a hasty manner and there were several errors in the original conclusions. At this point in time, it appears that the main question is a matter of making a decision as to whether you should discontinue the project, or the team should undertake and perform a new analysis.

We have enclosed for your information the details that resulted from the study. Due to the fact that the short amount of time is a factor in this situation, we would greatly appreciate your reviewing the information, and your reaching a decision and informing us of it, in a prompt way.

Check your revisions on the next page.

Your revisions should look something like this.

~~During the month of~~ <ins>In</ins> ∧March, ~~the people who are working on~~ the HUF
project team ∧<ins>studied</ins> ~~made a study of the past history of~~ HUF ∧<ins>'s history</ins> ~~in order~~ to
~~come to some conclusions as to~~ ∧<ins>decide</ins> whether ∧<ins>they had</ins> the ~~necessary~~ information
~~was available for the purpose of their~~ ∧<ins>necessary to</ins> ~~determining the project~~ ∧<ins>determine its</ins> ∧goals.

The ~~people who were~~ members of this study team ∧<ins>believe</ins> ~~are of the opinion~~
that the original analysis was done ∧<ins>hastily</ins> ~~in a hasty manner~~ and ∧<ins>that</ins> ∧there

were several errors in the original conclusions. ~~At this point in time,~~
~~it~~ ∧<ins>It</ins> appears ∧<ins>now</ins> that the main question is ~~a matter of making a decision~~

~~as to~~ whether you should discontinue the project, or the team should

undertake ~~and perform~~ a new analysis.

We have enclosed ~~for your information the details which resulted from~~
the study ∧<ins>results</ins>. ~~Due to the fact that the short amount of~~ ∧<ins>Since</ins> time is ~~a factor~~
~~in this situation~~ ∧<ins>short</ins>, we would greatly appreciate ~~your reviewing the in-~~
~~formation, and your reaching a decision and~~ ∧informing us ∧<ins>it if you</ins>
∧<ins>of your decision soon.</ins> ~~of it, in a prompt way.~~

Assignment

Read one or more of your writing samples. Select two or three sentences you think are cluttered and write them below. Then revise the sentences so they are more concise.

ORIGINAL

_____

_____

_____

_____

REVISION

_____

_____

_____

_____

ORIGINAL

_____

_____

_____

_____

REVISION

_____

_____

_____

_____

ORIGINAL

_____

_____

_____

_____

REVISION

_____

_____

_____

_____

REVIEW

To review what you've learned in this lesson, answer these questions.

1. _____ words are obstacles to good business writing. They clutter up your sentences, and slow your readers down.   (101)

2. Sometimes you can collapse several words or a long phrase into_____ that conveys your message quickly and clearly   (102)

3. Some sentences can be streamlined by removing unnecessary _____, _____, and _____ clauses.   (105)

4. Phrases like _____ _____ can clutter up sentences—either on their own, or by requiring extra words after the phrase.   (105)

WHAT'S NEXT?

In this lesson, you've examined ways to streamline your language to hold your readers' interest and save them time. In Lesson 4, you'll learn ways to make your sentences clearer.

4 USE CLEAR LANGUAGE

INTRODUCTION

Language should convey your message swiftly and accurately. Some writers try to impress their readers with unnecessarily complex language, which slows down and confuses readers more often than it impresses them.

Unnecessarily complex language can result in miscommunication, frustration, and wasted time. The most effective and impressive writing makes complex ideas seem simple and clear.

OBJECTIVES

In this lesson, you'll learn to write more professionally and effectively with these techniques:

- Using active language
- Using specific language
- Using plain English
- Avoiding jargon

Here is an e-mail written in language so vague, pompous, and passive that it's hard to tell what the writer wants to say.

> Dear Ms. Carelli:
>
> This is in reference to your recent e-mail which has been received and forwarded to the appropriate department.
>
> Please be advised that your complaint will be prioritized immediately and you will be contacted when the nature of the difficulty has been ascertained. Action will then be taken in accordance with the facts.
>
> We regret this unfortunate occurrence. Please do not hesitate to contact this writer if further assistance is required.
>
> Sincerely,
>
> Joyce Ellensby

Hard to follow, isn't it? Here's what the writer may have meant.

> Dear Ms. Carelli:
>
> Thank you for your e-mail. I am sorry we have misplaced your loan documents, delaying your loan approval.
>
> James Nguyen manages our Research Department; searching for your documents is a high priority for his team. He will send me a report within three days.
>
> I will call you by next Friday with an update on your application's status.
>
> Sincerely,
>
> Joyce Ellensby

The revised e-mail is more concise, even though it includes some new information. The new e-mail also gets the message across more clearly because the writer used active, specific language, with plain English instead of business jargon.

USE ACTIVE LANGUAGE

Passive language can weaken your writing, confuse your readers, and make your sentences longer. In contrast, active language focuses your readers' attention and increases the impact of your message.

As you can see in the following examples, in active language, the actor comes before the action. To use active language, say *who* acts, not just what the action is. The actor is underlined in the following revisions, and the action is boldfaced.

PASSIVE   The project **was managed** by John.

ACTIVE   John **managed** the project.
(unnecessary words: "was" and "by") (actor: John) (action: managed)

PASSIVE   The design document **has been completed** by the team.

ACTIVE   The team **has completed** the design document.

PASSIVE   A safety plan **was prepared and distributed** to employees by the committee.

ACTIVE   The committee **prepared** a safety plan and **distributed** it to employees.

When you give instructions, it is particularly important to say clearly what you want your readers to do. It can be frustrating and confusing to try to follow instructions that someone wrote in passive language.

PASSIVE   The water **should be measured** every 35 minutes.

ACTIVE   The technician **should measure** the water every 35 minutes.

—OR—

[*an implied you*] **Measure** the water every 35 minutes.

These revisions make the passive language active by implying or stating an actor before the action. Either the technician or the reader—"you"— should measure the water.

Sometimes the actor in a sentence is implied rather than spelled out. For instance, in the sentence "Prepare a safety plan," the implied subject is "you." (I.e., "I'm asking or telling you to prepare a safety plan.") The actor in a sentence isn't always a person: "The plan is flawed"; "The weather prevented us from going out."

PASSIVE   The cover of the printer **should be lifted,** the ink cartridges that **have been emptied should be removed,** and the new ink cartridges **should be opened, prepared, and inserted** in the appropriate slots.

ACTIVE   [*implied you*] **Lift** the printer cover, **remove** the empty cartridges, **open** and **prepare** the new cartridges, and **insert** them into the appropriate slot.

In this revision, the implied actor—an implied "you," or the reader—now appears before the action of lifting the cover and removing the cartridges.

The next two examples also show how to revise a passive-language sentence by adding a missing subject or actor.

PASSIVE   The door **was found** unlocked three times during the past month.

ACTIVE   <u>The security guard</u> **found** the door unlocked three times during the past month.

PASSIVE   It **would be appreciated** if the report **could be delivered** to me on Monday.

ACTIVE   <u>I</u> **would appreciate** it if <u>you</u> **deliver** the report to me on Monday.

> See the Verbs section of Lesson 5: Grammar for a more complete discussion of passive and active language, including situations when passive language may be appropriate.

PRACTICE

Revise these sentences so they are active, direct, and clear. The first step is to identify an actor. (Feel free to invent one.)

1. The research project is being conducted by the News Department.

   _____

   _____

   _____

   _____

2. A copy of the approval must be stapled to the request before it is forwarded to the Accounting Office.

_____

_____

_____

_____

3. The new design is attached for your review and its return by March 15 would be appreciated.

_____

_____

_____

_____

4. An investigation will be conducted by Andrea Russo into the concern voiced by Mr. Szabo.

_____

_____

_____

_____

5. Reservations for the conference can be made by telephoning Tom Woo at Extension 4732 before December 1.

_____

_____

_____

_____

Your revisions should look something like these; the more active, revised words are boldfaced here. Make sure that the actor comes before the action in your revisions.

1: ORIGINAL   The research project is being conducted by the News Department.

REVISION   **The News Department is conducting** the research project.

2: ORIGINAL   A copy of the approval must be stapled to the request before it is forwarded to the Accounting Office.

REVISION   **You must staple** a copy of the approval to the request before **forwarding** it to the Accounting Office.

3: ORIGINAL   The new design is attached for your review and its return by March 15 would be appreciated.

REVISION   [*an implied you*] Please **review** the design and **return** it by March 15.

4: ORIGINAL   An investigation will be conducted by Andrea Russo into the concern voiced by Mr. Szabo.

REVISION   **Mr. Szabo voiced** a concern and **Andrea Russo will investigate** it.

5: ORIGINAL   Reservations for the conference can be made by telephoning Tom Woo at Extension 4732 before December 1.

REVISION   **You can make** reservations for the conference by **telephoning** Tom Woo at Extension 4732 before December 1.

—OR—

REVISION   [*implied you*] **To make** reservations for the conference, **telephone** Tom Woo at Extension 4732 before December 1.

Assignment

Do you use too much passive language when you write? Look through your own writing for passive, indirect sentences. If you find any, write two of them below. Then revise the sentences so they are active and direct. If you don't find any passive sentences, go on to the next section of this lesson.

If you're not sure whether a sentence is passive or active, underline the actor and circle the action. The language is passive if you can't find an actor (including an implied "you") or if the actor comes after the action.

ORIGINAL

_____

_____

_____

_____

REVISION

_____

_____

_____

_____

ORIGINAL

_____

_____

_____

_____

REVISION

_____

_____

_____

USE SPECIFIC LANGUAGE

Specific language makes your writing easier to read, while vague language paints an unclear picture. The more specific your language is, the less guesswork and effort your readers will need to understand your message.

VAGUE   **Some time ago,** the **building** was destroyed **in a disaster**.

SPECIFIC   In 1994, fire destroyed the apartment house.

VAGUE   Our **group went** to Los Angeles **for a meeting**.

SPECIFIC   Our project team flew to Los Angeles to meet with Harriet Allen, the system designer.

VAGUE   Ask the client to complete the **paperwork** in **a timely manner**.

SPECIFIC   Ask the client to complete the new account application form within ten working days.

It can show consideration when you supply your readers with precise information. Vague language can require them to guess at unknown meanings behind your word choices, so try using words and phrases like the ones listed here to make your writing less vague and more specific.

VAGUE	SPECIFIC
vehicle	car
car	convertible
equipment	computer
computer	laptop
went	walked; ran; drove
traveled	flew; took the train; sailed
contacted	called; spoke to; visited
proper	correct; easy-to-use
some	five
recently	yesterday
in a timely manner	by August 15; within two weeks

PRACTICE

Underline the vague, general words and phrases in these sentences. Then use your imagination to fill in details and revise the sentences so they communicate specific, useful information.

1. Recently, we looked at a structure that might be suitable for our needs.

   _____

   _____

   _____

2. During the incident, Ms. Brown sustained multiple injuries to her upper torso and limbs.

   _____

   _____

   _____

3. We have identified a few items to be discussed at the meeting, so please leave considerable time in your schedule.

   _____

   _____

   _____

   _____

Here are some possible revisions; yours will be different because you added different details. The original boldfaced words are vague and imprecise; here are more concrete terms to replace them.

1: ORIGINAL   **Recently**, we looked at a **structure** that might be **suitable** for our **needs**.

REVISION   Last week we looked at a four-story building that might be big enough for our new machine polishers.

2: ORIGINAL   During the **incident**, Ms. Brown **sustained multiple injuries** to her **upper torso and limbs**.

REVISION   During the fall, Ms. Brown's chest, shoulders, and arms were scratched and cut.

3: ORIGINAL   We have identified **a few items** to be discussed at the meeting, so please leave **considerable time** in your schedule.

REVISION   At the meeting, we will discuss the next conference, the move to the new building, and the new staff position, so please leave at least three hours in your schedule.

Assignment

Check your own writing to see whether you have used vague words and phrases. Underline any words or phrases you find and write them below. Revise two of them to be more specific and clear.

ORIGINAL

_____

_____

_____

REVISION

_____

_____

_____

ORIGINAL

_____

_____

_____

REVISION

_____

_____

_____

USE PLAIN ENGLISH

Do you ever have to read something very slowly because the writer has used unnecessarily formal language, or has used uncommon words when everyday words would have gotten the point across?

Pompous language can confuse, intimidate, amuse, or annoy your readers. Plain English communicates your message more reliably. Stuffy words and phrases can force readers to mentally translate your writing into everyday language, which can waste valuable time and create misunderstandings.

How long does it take for you to read this paragraph and understand it?

> Per your request, enclosed herewith are documents concerning the above-mentioned project. Please review said documents and return them to this office prior to January 15. We will then initiate the process of implementing the requested system modifications.

See how much easier the paragraph is to read when it's written in plain English?

> As you asked, I am sending a description of the Acme project. Please read the description and send it back to me before January 15. We will then start the system modifications.

Pompous language does not improve communication; instead, it gets in the way of your message. So use plain English when you write. Choose ordinary words that communicate your message as simply and directly as possible.

PRACTICE

Sometimes, the words in this list are the best, most precise words to use. But writers often use these words when simpler language would communicate more clearly. What ordinary words or phrases would be good alternatives to the words listed here? Use a thesaurus or dictionary if you're not sure.

1. prior to _____

2. subsequent to _____

3. utilize _____

4. modifications _____

5. enhance _____

6. beneficial _____

7. supplemental _____

8. magnitude _____

9. supersede _____

10. augment _____

11. heretofore _____

12. parameters _____

13. commence _____

14. endeavor _____

15. optimal _____

16. forthwith _____

Here are some possible replacement words. You may have different, equally correct answers.

1. prior to   before
2. subsequent to   after; following
3. utilize   use
4. modifications   changes
5. enhance   improve
6. beneficial   helpful
7. supplemental   extra
8. magnitude   size
9. supersede   replace
10. augment   increase; add to
11. heretofore   before; until now
12. parameters   boundaries; limits
13. commence   begin; start
14. endeavor   try
15. optimal   best; most favorable
16. forthwith   immediately

PRACTICE

Revise these sentences, using plain English and active language.

1. Division managers are hereupon requested to facilitate the implementation of the afore-mentioned program by forwarding details of their personnel requirements.

   _____

   _____

   _____

   _____

2. The injuries sustained by the passengers during the accident were the result of their failure to use the vehicle's restraining elements.

   _____

   _____

   _____

   _____

3. Enclosed herewith is a heretofore-unseen listing of procedures that must be implemented by our team immediately.

   _____

   _____

   _____

   _____

ANSWERS

Your revisions might look something like these.

1: ORIGINAL Division managers are hereupon requested to facilitate the implementation of the aforementioned program by forwarding details of their personnel requirements.

REVISION Please help us get this program started by letting us know how many people you need to complete the job.

—OR—

To help us get this program off the ground, please send us a list of your division's personnel needs.

2: ORIGINAL The injuries sustained by the passengers during the accident were the result of their failure to use the vehicle's restraining elements.

REVISION The passengers were injured in the accident because they didn't use seat belts.

3: ORIGINAL Enclosed herewith is a heretofore-unseen listing of procedures that must be implemented by our team immediately.

REVISION Here is a list of new procedures that our team must implement immediately.

—OR—

Please begin using these procedures at once.

Assignment

Look for examples of pompous language in your own writing. Underline any words or phrases you find and write them below. Revise two of them, using plain English.

ORIGINAL

_____

_____

_____

_____

REVISION

_____

_____

_____

_____

ORIGINAL

_____

_____

_____

REVISION

_____

_____

_____

_____

**Next, look at the importance of using
plain English instead of jargon when you write.**

AVOID JARGON

Business writing is full of business jargon—words, phrases, abbreviations, and acronyms that make sense only to people who are used to business language, or who share a particular job.

Sometimes businesspeople give new meanings to familiar words, and sometimes they invent new jargon terms. Some of these terms enter mainstream language: bankers' automated teller machines from the 1970s are today's ATMs. *Networking* is another business term that has become widespread and very useful.

However, jargon damages business writing when it's difficult or impossible for the reader to understand. Use plain English instead of jargon when you write to someone who may not recognize general business jargon, or terms that are specific to your job. Define any term that may be new to your reader. Here are a few examples of business jargon that a reader might find confusing:

> **bullish on:** confident of success in a given activity
>
> **going forward:** in the future
>
> **push the envelope:** to go beyond usual limits
>
> **put a pin in it:** "Hold that thought" or "Let's come back to that later"

Here are three kinds of jargon you should usually avoid:

1. Everyday words used in a nonstandard way:

   > We plan a campaign to **migrate** customers to our bank.

2. Words your reader won't find in a current dictionary:

   > We hope to **maximalize** our marketing potential.

3. Potentially unclear acronyms:

   > Next year's goals include increasing the **BOCSF,** establishing a **RADIT,** and improving the **FAJ.**

If you use an acronym, spell out the words the first time you use the term, followed by the acronym in parentheses. Afterward, just use the acronym. For instance, the following sentences could be part of an e-mail to a new intern in an office:

> I'd like you to read the attached request for proposal (RFP). Let's discuss the RFP on Monday; after that, I'd like you to start writing a response to it.

PRACTICE

Look for examples of jargon in your own writing. If you find any, underline the words and then write them below. Translate two of the jargon words into plain English.

JARGON

_____

TRANSLATION

_____

JARGON

_____

TRANSLATION

_____

PRACTICE

To apply what you learned in this lesson, revise the following paragraphs so the language is active, specific, and in plain English. Invent any details you like.

> Enclosed herewith is the information requested by you in your recent communication with the undersigned subsequent to your recent purchase of our computer system. It is our belief that the enhancements described therein would be beneficial to the efficiency of your organization by making it possible to increase the amount of data processed within a given time period.
>
> It is our policy to endeavor to provide the optimum service possible to our customers. Please be advised that should you have additional questions or concerns, every attempt will be made to provide a response in a timely manner.

_____

_____

_____

_____

_____

_____

_____

_____

_____

_____

_____

_____

ANSWER

Here is one way to revise the paragraphs. The details of your revision will differ.

As you asked, I am sending a description of the improvements we plan to make to the Model 603A computer system you purchased from us last year. We believe these improvements will help your organization process at least 15 percent more data each month.

We try to provide the best possible service to our customers. Please let me know if you have any more questions or concerns, and I will do my best to address them within five working days.

REVIEW

Fill in the blanks with the correct word or phrase. If you're not sure, check the page number after the sentence.

1. In active language, the _____ comes before the _____.   (117)

2. _____ makes your writing easier to read, while vague language paints an unclear picture.   (122)

3. Pompous language can confuse, intimidate, amuse, or annoy your readers. _____ communicates your message more reliably.   (126)

4. Business writing is full of business _____—that is, words, phrases, abbreviations, and acronyms that make sense only to people who are used to business language or who share a particular job.   (132)

WHAT'S NEXT?

In this lesson, you've examined ways to use language to communicate more actively, simply, and clearly. In Lesson 5, you'll learn how to ensure that your grammar is correct for any business document you write.

5 USE CORRECT GRAMMAR

INTRODUCTION

American English can be difficult to write correctly because it doesn't always follow clear-cut rules. You might find differences between the advice in this book and another book's advice, or the rules you learned in school. That's because many grammar and word-usage issues are not matters of hard-and-fast rules, but of style. Throughout this workbook, you'll find widely accepted and easy-to-use style guidelines that are accepted in the workplace today.

OBJECTIVES

In this lesson, you'll learn to write clearly and professionally with these strategies:

- Avoiding incomplete sentences and achieving parallel sentence structure

- Using strategic parts of speech to write clear, correct, dynamic sentences

- Recognizing the effects of passive and active language, and using them appropriately

- Recognizing frequently misused words, and using them appropriately and confidently

INCOMPLETE SENTENCES AND PARALLEL STRUCTURE

First, you'll learn how to avoid incomplete sentences and maintain parallel structure in a sentence. These techniques make sure that each sentence you write communicates a complete thought to a reader, and make sure that the reader grasps the logic of your message.

INCOMPLETE SENTENCES

A complete sentence contains a subject and a verb, and it conveys at least one complete thought.

An incomplete sentence ends in a period, but the writer has omitted information that the reader needs. Some incomplete sentences are missing a subject or verb, or both.

Circle the numbers in front of the incomplete sentences here.

1.   Always arrives on time.

2.   Because she is usually reliable.

3.   The results of inaccurate accounting practices.

4.   Until after the final day of the conference.

You should have circled all the numbers. They are all incomplete sentences.

INCOMPLETE   A few hours.

COMPLETE   It will take a few hours.

Sometimes a complete sentence becomes incomplete when you add another word.

COMPLETE   Janine has returned from Chicago.

INCOMPLETE   Because Janine has returned from Chicago.

COMPLETE   We're happy because Janine has returned from Chicago.

Incomplete sentences like the middle example are often the result of a writer's beginning a thought, becoming distracted, and forgetting to complete it. Proofreading your work will help you catch unfinished thoughts and incomplete sentences like these.

For more tips on complete versus incomplete sentences, see Lesson 7: Write Effective E-Mail, page 217.

PARALLEL STRUCTURE

To help your writing flow smoothly and make sense, use the same format for items you present in a series. A series with items in different formats makes a sentence awkward to read. As the reader scans through a series with parallel structure, the relationships between different pieces of information are clear.

NOT PARALLEL At the February meeting we will **hold a discussion of** the new health plan, **whether to revise** the procedures manual, and then **a draft will be developed of** the early retirement policy.

PARALLEL At the February meeting, we will **discuss** the new health plan, **decide** whether to revise the procedures manual, and **draft** an early retirement policy.

These parallel verb tenses save space and help guide the reader smoothly through the plans for the February meeting.

PRACTICE

Underline structures in these sentences that either are parallel or should be parallel. If necessary, rewrite the sentences.

1. Rita's responsibilities include sorting the mail, answering the phone, and to run errands.

   _____

   _____

   _____

   _____

2. We have asked managers to reduce travel budgets by 20 percent and that expense reports should be submitted weekly.

   _____

   _____

   _____

   _____

3. During my annual trip to Asia, I plan to visit our office in Japan, meet with officials in South Korea, look at possible manufacturing sites in China, and explore the possibility of setting up operations in Vietnam.

   _____

   _____

   _____

   _____

Check your answers on the next page.

ANSWERS

The parallel words are underlined, and the revised words are in bold.

1. Rita's responsibilities include <u>sorting</u> the mail, <u>answering</u> the phone, and **<u>running</u>** errands.

2. We have asked managers <u>to reduce</u> travel budgets by 20 percent and **<u>to submit</u>** expense reports weekly.

3. *(correct)* During my annual trip to Asia, I <u>planned to visit</u> our office in Japan, <u>meet</u> with officials in South Korea, <u>look</u> at possible manufacturing sites in China, and <u>explore</u> the possibility of setting up operations in Vietnam.

PRONOUNS

These two kinds of pronoun mistakes are common in business writing:

- Unclear pronouns
- Gender-biased pronouns

UNCLEAR PRONOUNS

As you can see from these examples, unclear pronouns quickly confuse readers.

UNCLEAR   When Marta met with Susan Garcia last week, <u>she</u> agreed to accept the revised proposal.

CLEAR   Susan Garcia agreed to accept the revised proposal when she met with Marta last week.

UNCLEAR   The transit officials plan to increase fares to reduce the annual deficit. <u>This</u> will be a hardship for commuters.

CLEAR   Transit officials plan to increase fares to reduce the annual deficit. This increase will be a hardship for commuters.

UNCLEAR   Tom's shirt stopped fitting his waistline, so he had <u>it</u> taken in.

CLEAR   Tom had his shirt taken in to fit his waistline.

PRACTICE

See if you can clear up the confusing pronouns in these sentences. Feel free to guess the writer's meaning.

1. The catalog had a picture of the work station the company needed, so Alex decided to buy it.

    _____

    _____

    _____

    _____

2. Ellen was unable to finish the project on time and explained the problem to Brandi. She was very frustrated.

    _____

    _____

    _____

    _____

    _____

Check your answers on the next page.

POSSIBLE REVISIONS

1. Alex decided to buy the catalog because it had a picture of the work station the company needed.

—OR—

Because the company needed a work station, Alex decided to buy the one pictured in the catalog.

2. Ellen was unable to finish the project on time and explained the problem to Brandi. Brandi was very frustrated.

—OR—

Brandi was very frustrated when she learned Ellen was unable to finish the project on time.

GENDER-BIASED PRONOUNS

In grammar, the term *gender* refers to the way a language categorizes words as feminine, masculine, or neutral:

- <u>She</u> received <u>her</u> law degree in 1995.

- <u>His</u> ambition was to ride <u>his</u> bicycle across the country.

- <u>It's</u> a beautiful building.

Until the late 1960s, it was common practice to use masculine pronouns—*he*, *his*, and *him*—to refer to both women and men. Today, however, it's no longer acceptable to use masculine pronouns for groups that include women.

GENDER-   The administrative assistant asked everyone to select <u>his</u> preferred option by the
BIASED   first of next month.

The most effective way to remove gender bias is to revise the sentence, using plural nouns and pronouns.

REVISED   The administrative assistant asked <u>all employees</u> to select <u>their</u> preferred <u>options</u> by the first of next month.

It has become more acceptable to use the plural pronouns *their* and *them* with singular indefinite pronouns such as *everyone*. But whenever you can, try to phrase sentences to avoid gender bias without using awkward constructions or clumsy grammar.

AWKWARD	The administrative assistant asked everyone to select <u>his/her</u> preferred health provider option by the first of next month.
AWKWARD	The administrative assistant asked everyone to select the health provider option <u>s/he</u> prefers by the first of next month.
CLUMSY GRAMMAR	The administrative assistant asked everyone to select <u>their</u> preferred health provider option by the first of next month.
UNBIASED AND CORRECT	The administrative assistant asked <u>all of us</u> to select <u>our</u> preferred health provider <u>options</u> by the first of next month.

PRACTICE

Revise these sentences to remove gender bias.

1. This weekend, somebody left the lights on in his apartment.

   _____

   _____

   _____

2. When compiling figures for the audit, an accountant should always make sure she has the most recent figures.

   _____

   _____

   _____

Check your answers on the next page.

ANSWERS

1. Lights were left on in one apartment over the weekend.

—OR—

The lights stayed on in one apartment over the weekend.

2. When compiling figures for the audit, accountants should always make sure they have the most recent figures.

Assignment

Review your own writing samples for unclear pronoun references or gender-biased pronouns. If you find any, write the sentences below and then revise them. If you don't find any examples, go on to the next section.

ORIGINAL

_____

_____

_____

_____

REVISION

_____

_____

_____

_____

ORIGINAL

_____

_____

_____

REVISION

_____

_____

_____

_____

SUBJECT-VERB AGREEMENT

It's sometimes hard to know whether to use the singular or the plural form of a verb. Circle the numbers in front of the sentences that use correct verb tenses:

1. Each of the systems are failing.

2. Mr. Bruce and Mr. Appleby has received the e-mail.

3. One of the calculators was advertised at a reduced price.

4. The decision of the judges are final.

5. Neither of the clerks wants to change the hours.

6. Four dollars are not enough to buy us all coffee.

The verb tenses are correct in Sentences 3 and 5.

On the next few pages you'll find some of the basic rules that ensure subject-verb agreement in your sentences.

A plural noun takes a singular verb when it conveys a single expression of time, money, or another quantity. The subjects are underlined and the verbs are boldfaced in this lesson.

EXAMPLES   Ninety-nine cents **isn't** much to pay for a song.

Three blocks **feels** like a long way to walk in some parts of this town.

Six hours **is** enough time for me to finish it.

It's best to use a singular verb after these pronouns:

anyone	everyone	nothing
anything	everything	one (of)
each	neither	some
either	nobody	somebody
every	no one	someone
everybody	none	something

EXAMPLES   One of the four systems **is** problematic.

Every agent, supervisor, and floor manager **is** needed.

No one **wants** to do the chore.

Somebody **has** to revise the protocols.

Two or more singular subjects joined by *and* take a plural verb.

EXAMPLE   <u>Pencil and paper</u> **are** required for the test.

When a noun is the subject of a sentence, the verb agrees with the noun—even if the subject is followed by other nouns.

EXAMPLE   <u>The use</u> of BlackBerries and phones **is** prohibited during staff meetings.

In this example, the singular noun "use" is the subject of the sentence. It takes priority over "BlackBerries and phones," and takes a single noun. If the subject of that sentence were plural, it would take a plural verb.

EXAMPLE   <u>Exits</u> from the room to answer Blackberries and phones **are** prohibited during staff meetings.

If you're struggling over what verb tense sounds best, then **try rewriting the sentence.** An implied subject "you" agrees with the verb in this revised sentence: "Do not use phones or BlackBerries during staff meetings." This sentence is also much easier to understand than either of the examples above.

When a noun is the subject of a sentence, the verb agrees with the noun—even when it's followed by other nouns and a phrase like *as well as*, *along with*, or *in addition to*.

EXAMPLE   <u>Sheila</u>, with the enthusiastic support of Roberta and Jim, **plans** to protest the new restrictions.

In that case, Sheila is the subject of the sentence. The singular subject takes a singular verb.

The same rule applies to sentences with other words that come between the subject and the verb.

EXAMPLE   <u>The largest building</u> on the corner where Main St., Fourth St., and Second Ave. intersect **has** always appealed to me.

In this case, "on the corner where Main St., Fourth St., and Second Ave. intersect" is as irrelevant as Roberta and Jim's enthusiastic support in the earlier sentence. The building has always appealed to the writer. The singular subject takes a singular verb no matter how many words pile up in the space between.

If that sentence started, "The buildings," plural, then the verb would be plural to match the plural buildings: "<u>The buildings</u> on the corner where Main St., Fourth St., and Second Ave. intersect **have** always appealed to me."

Practice subject-verb agreement on the next page.

PRACTICE

Underline the correct verb in each sentence.

1. The purpose of his requests (was, were) to get the additional funds.

2. I don't think either of the new designs (are, is) going to last for a year.

3. Each computer, desk, and printer (is, are) marked down

4. The cause of the errors (is, are) unknown.

5. One of the reasons for absences (is, are) poor health.

6. The largest of the three banks (is, are) in Petaluma.

7. Everyone I asked, including the managers of both locations, (agree, agrees) with my decision.

Check your answers on the next page.

ANSWERS

1. The purpose of his requests <u>was</u> to get the additional funds.

2. I don't think either of the new designs <u>is</u> going to last for a year.

3. Each computer, desk, and printer <u>is</u> marked down.

4. The cause of the errors <u>is</u> unknown.

5. One of the reasons for absences <u>is</u> poor health.

6. The largest of the three banks <u>is</u> in Petaluma.

7. Everyone I asked, including the managers of both locations, <u>agrees</u> with my decision.

PASSIVE LANGUAGE AND HIDDEN VERBS

You learned in Lesson 4 how passive language can make your writing unclear. Many grammar experts strongly condemn passive language, but many writers still use it. For most business writing, passive language will weaken your sentences and confuse your readers.

However, there are times when passive language is appropriate. This section gives you some questions to ask as you decide when and whether to use it.

Active language propels a sentence forward by harnessing its verbs; in this section, you'll also learn how to unlock verbs from passive language. Your sentences will become more clear, concise, and energetic.

PASSIVE AND ACTIVE LANGUAGE

Passive language is sometimes acceptable. But whenever you use passive language, you should do it consciously and carefully, and because it fits the sentence better than active language. Save passive construction only for situations when the person or thing taking an action is unknown, or not important.

Passive language often obscures who takes an action, while active language clearly reveals who does what in a sentence. Sometimes a sentence names a person who takes an action, but the sentence is still couched in passive language.

EXAMPLE   <u>Thousands of dollars</u> **were saved** for the company by Antoine's timely idea.

This sentence wastes space and downplays Antoine's accomplishment. Active language corrects these problems.

REVISION   <u>Antoine</u> **saved** the company thousands of dollars with his timely idea.

Sometimes a sentence implies who takes an action or holds an opinion, but the sentence is still in passive language.

EXAMPLE   Jill explained that business suits are considered unnecessary in this office.

This writer implies that all the people who work in the office recognize a shared rule about appropriate office clothes. It may be unimportant who holds this view. Nevertheless, the sentence is simpler and stronger in the active voice:

REVISED   Jill explained that no one considers business suits necessary in this office.

PRACTICE

Examine the passive language in the following sentences. Revise them, feeling free to add details, if you think active language would improve the sentences. Underline the action, and who takes the action.

1.   Safety regulations had not been observed by the setup crew.

2.   The document was hyphenated automatically.

3.   Sales declined that quarter, as they were expected to do.

Check your answers on the next page.

ANSWERS

1. The <u>setup crew</u> **had not observed** safety regulations.

2. The document was **hyphenated** automatically. (*fine as it is, since a computer takes the action*)

3. Sales declined that quarter, as <u>analysts</u> **had expected**.

Turn the page to learn other ways to make your language more active.

VERBS FROZEN IN NOUN FORMS

Passive constructions often freeze the real action of a sentence behind a noun and two unnecessary, passive verbs. In these cases, it saves space and improves the sentence to translate the action from a noun into a verb.

EXAMPLE The suggestion <u>was made</u> that we go.

REVISION Vikram <u>suggested</u> that we go.

The passive verb "was made" adds unnecessary bulk to the sentence, and the verb *to make* doesn't represent the most important action. By examining the noun "suggestion" you can find another, implied verb and the sentence's real action: *to suggest*.

Sentences can be written in active language, but still contain verbs frozen in noun forms. These sentences often feature stale, everyday verbs like "to be" that don't represent the sentences' real action. Sometimes an *-ing* noun form of a verb slows these sentences down.

EXAMPLE <u>Her singing</u> **is** amazingly good.

REVISION <u>She</u> **sings** amazingly well.

This revision replaces the stale verb "is" with the more interesting verb "sings." The new sentence is crisper because the words "She sings" identify the actor and action much more simply and energetically than the words "Her singing is . . . ."

PRACTICE

Practice releasing verbs from noun forms in the following exercise. Feel free to add words and ideas to rewrite the sentences to be shorter and more direct.

1. Our preference is that you act immediately.

    _____

    _____

    _____

    _____

2. Eating, drinking, and smoking are prohibited on all transit vehicles.

    _____

    _____

    _____

    _____

3. The demonstration of project-management skills is a requirement for all applicants.

    _____

    _____

    _____

    _____

Check your answers on the next page.

ANSWERS

1. <u>We</u> **prefer** that you act immediately.

2. <u>You</u> **may not** eat, drink, or smoke on transit vehicles.

3. <u>We</u> **require** that all applicants demonstrate project-management skills.

—OR—

<u>All applicants</u> **must demonstrate** project-management skills.

FREQUENTLY MISUSED WORDS

Many English words sound alike but have different meanings and spellings, which sometimes makes it hard to avoid misusing words. Here are two methods that can help you use the right words:

- Rewrite the sentence, using a word that's easier to recognize
- Memorize the differences between similar-sounding words

USE A DIFFERENT WORD

Try rewriting the sentence below with a word that isn't as easy to confuse with a similar word.

> Nick met with his supervisor for (**advise / advice**) about ways to handle a troublesome customer.

The right word is *advice*, but you could also use *suggestions*.

> Nick met with his supervisor for **suggestions** about ways to handle a troublesome customer.

MEMORIZE THE DIFFERENCES BETWEEN SIMILAR-SOUNDING WORDS

Here are some pairs of useful word that people often confuse because they look or sound similar. Memorizing the differences between them will give you more options when you write.

accept / except	lead / led
access / excess	loose / lose
advice / advise	maybe / may be
affect / effect	personal / personnel
already / all ready	principal / principle
choose / chose	than / then
cite / sight / site	

Also, *alright* has its own entry in *Merriam-Webster's Eleventh Collegiate Dictionary*, but you should always spell it as two words: *all right*. Many readers will assume you made a spelling mistake if you use the one-word form.

You can't count on your spell-check or grammar-check features to catch misused words. In fact, these easily mistaken words often crop up as errors in newspapers and on news sites that rely on computers instead of human proofreaders.

On the following pages are definitions and some mnemonic devices to help you remember which word to use for a given situation.

accept / except

We **accept** your offer with great pleasure.	verb: to receive or to agree
Sandy is good at everything **except** totaling the figures.	other than

TO REMEMBER: **Accept** and **agree** both start with *a*.

---

access / excess

The new road gives us **access** to our property.	way of getting to
This pass guarantees **access** to the concert.	permission to enter
The new attorney has an **excess** of energy.	too much

TO REMEMBER: The "**ex**" in **excess** sounds like **extra**.

---

advice / advise

I'd appreciate your **advice** about which system to purchase.	noun: recommendation, help
We were called in to **advise** the company about ways to trim the budget.	verb: to give advice

---

affect / effect

The delay will not **affect** our ability to meet the deadline.	verb: to change
One **effect** of the fire was that we lost five years' worth of records.	noun: a result

already / all ready

The game is **already** over.	before a given time
The drivers are **all ready** to leave.	all prepared

As a separate word, *all* refers to several people or objects. If you can place a noun between *all* and *ready*, as in the sentence "**All** <u>the drivers are</u> **ready** to leave," use the two separate words—*all ready*—rather than the single word *already*.

---

alright / all right

"The first two years of medical school were **alright**." —Gertrude Stein	a highly controversial spelling
That was a nasty fall: are you **all right**?	the unarguably correct spelling

In short, *alright*'s wrong. *All right* is two words.

---

choose / chose

Each department can **choose** the colors for its own offices.	present or future tense of the verb *to choose*
We **chose** Honolulu as the site of its next meeting.	past tense of the verb *to choose*

cite / sight / site

The attorney **cited** similar cases.	verb: to quote or refer to
She travels because she loves each new **sight.**	noun: something seen
The new jail will be built on the **site.**	noun: location, piece of land, place on the Web

TO REMEMBER:

- **Cite** is from the word **citation.**
- **Sight** is spelled like **light.** Both words refer to something you can see.

---

lead / led

Be sure to place a **lead** apron on the patient's lap for X-rays.	noun: metal
The facilitator **led** the discussion.	past tense of the verb *to lead*
Do they **lead** the discussions?	present or future tense of the verb *to lead*

---

loose / lose

Please put your **loose** change into the coffee fund.	not contained
The wheel wobbles because it is **loose.**	not securely attached
Unfortunately, we continue to **lose** customers.	verb: to have fewer, or to have less

TO REMEMBER: Lost is the past tense of **lose**—only the final letter changes.

maybe / may be

Maybe we should talk again on Thursday.   perhaps

This **may be** our last chance to change the   verb: is possibly
logo on our cards.

TO REMEMBER:

- **Maybe** is one word when you're **uncertain** about something.

- Use **may be** as two words when you could add the word *well* between them: "This **may** <u>well</u> **be** our last chance."

---

personal / personnel

Benefits include one day of **personal** time   belonging to an individual
every four months.

All newly hired **personnel** are required   employees
to attend an orientation meeting.

TO REMEMBER: Personnel has the same *e* as **employees.**

---

principal / principle

Tomás is our first choice for school   chief, head
principal.

The **principal** reason for her dismissal was   primary, most important
her high rate of absenteeism.

He has paid off the **principal** and the interest   a financial term
from the mortgage.

Because of her **principles**, she would not   rules of conduct
approve the illegal use of funds.

TO REMEMBER:

- A **pal** and a **principal** are two kinds of people.

- **Principle** ends with *e*; **ethics** begins with *e*.

---

than / then

After accepting congratulations for his sales record, Isaac **then** graciously thanked his associates.	at that time
Anik can complete her statistical assessments faster **than** anyone else in the department.	the word sets up a comparison

TO REMEMBER: Then is spelled like **when**, and both words refer to time.

For brief, enjoyable tips on grammar and word usage, look up Mignon Fogarty's *Grammar Girl* podcast. You can also read and play episodes on her website at grammar.quickand-dirtytips.com. Her topics include the distinctions between *lay* and *lie*; *assure*, *ensure*, and *insure*; *will* and *shall*; and *who* and *whom*. She also covers issues like "How to Write a Great Blog Comment."

Turn the page for some practice.

PRACTICE

Circle the correct word or words to complete each sentence.

1. If all goes well, next year's budget will include funds for a significant increase in the number of employees in the (personal / personnel) department.

2. Everyone on the team believes that Davida is a more competent administrator (then / than) Eugene is.

3. The small (principal / principle) sum accrues little interest.

4. The drop in the stock market will have no (affect / effect) on our plans for expansion.

5. We are (already / all ready) two months late with our loan payment.

6. He has a tendency to ask for too much (advise / advice).

7. Earlier, she (led / lead) the dog out into the yard.

8. The inspectors found that the safety rules were far too (lose / loose).

9. Her test performance was (alright / all right).

Check your answers on the next page.

ANSWERS

1. If all goes well, next year's budget will include funds for a significant increase in the number of employees in the <u>personnel</u> department.

2. Everyone on the team believes that Davida is a more competent administrator <u>than</u> Eugene is.

3. The small <u>principal</u> sum accrues little interest.

4. The drop in the stock market will have no <u>effect</u> on our plans for expansion.

5. We are <u>already</u> two months late with our loan payment.

6. He has a tendency to ask for too much <u>advice</u>.

7. Earlier, she <u>led</u> the dog out into the yard.

8. The inspectors found that the safety rules were far too <u>loose</u>.

9. Her test performance was <u>all right</u>.

Assignment

Review your own writing sample for any subject-verb agreement errors and misused words. Use the space below to revise any incorrect sentences.

ORIGINAL

_____

_____

_____

_____

REVISION

_____

_____

_____

_____

ORIGINAL

_____

_____

_____

_____

REVISION

_____

_____

_____

_____

REVIEW

To review what you've learned in this lesson, answer these questions.

1. A complete sentence contains a _____ and a _____, and it conveys at least one _____. (138)

2. A plural noun takes a _____ verb tense when it conveys a single expression of time, money, or another quantity. (150)

3. Two or more singular subjects joined by *and* take a _____ verb. (151)

4. _____ language often obscures who takes an action, while _____ language clearly reveals who does what in a sentence. (155)

5. The spelling *alright* is _____ correct. (164)

WHAT'S NEXT?

In this lesson, you've learned how to ensure that your grammar is correct for any business document you write. In Lesson 6, you'll learn the correct uses of various punctuation marks.

6   USE CORRECT PUNCTUATION

INTRODUCTION

Punctuation mistakes distract your readers and reduce your credibility. No workbook can offer comprehensive coverage of punctuation in the American workplace: our language is too complex, and it changes too quickly. Nevertheless, this lesson will help you review punctuation rules that many business writers neglect.

OBJECTIVES

In this lesson, you'll learn to write clearly and professionally with these guidelines:

- Using punctuation marks to correct run-on sentences
- Using strategic punctuation marks correctly

PUNCTUATION AND RUN-ON SENTENCES

To start with a grammar term, a **clause** is any set of words within a sentence that contains its own subject and predicate. Clauses are the building blocks of correct and incorrect sentences, including run-on sentences.

See if you can underline the final clauses here:

> I got the job through Ms. Bucholz, who is a family friend.

> I remember that he joined the firm in September.

You recognized the final clauses if you underlined "who is a family friend" and "that he joined the firm in September."

A **run-on sentence** contains two or more clauses that are connected incorrectly. The clauses lack one of the following, necessary links:

- A conjunction such as *and, or, but, because* (etc.)

  —AND/OR—

- The right punctuation

Run-on sentences are not necessarily long, and some run-on sentences have no punctuation at all. (An example might be "Arrive on time leave on time.")

Here are two other kinds of run-on sentences:

1. Two complete sentences joined only with a comma:

   > The office will not be open over the <u>holiday, please</u> complete all important work by the day before.

2. Two complete sentences joined only with a comma and a word like *however, therefore,* or *meanwhile*:

   > The office will not be open over the <u>holiday, therefore please</u> complete all important work by the day before.

Here are four ways to correct a run-on sentence:

1. Use a period to divide the sentence into two or more new sentences:

   The office will not be open over the <u>holiday. Please</u> complete all important work by the day before.

2. Use a comma and a conjunction such as *and, or, but, because,* etc.:

   The office will not be open over the <u>holiday, so please</u> complete all important work by the day before.

3. Use a semicolon on its own:

   The office will not be open over the <u>holiday; please</u> complete all important work by the day before.

4. Use a semicolon and a word such as *however, therefore, meanwhile, also,* etc.:

   The office will not be open over the <u>holiday; therefore, please</u> complete all important work by the day before.

PRACTICE

Identify the run-on sentences below, and put an **X** beside them. Then use any of the methods explained earlier to correct them.

	RUN-ON?
ORIGINAL We met for six hours, however, we could not reach a consensus.	**X**
REVISION We met for six hours; however, we could not reach a consensus.	_____

1. The agency completed the investigation last month; its findings were inconclusive.

   _____

2. We believe the problem is separate, it is not related to the earlier fire.

   _____

3. She has received the most up-to-date treatment, her depression hinders her recovery.

   _____

4. Let me know if you would like to meet with our team; meanwhile, we will proceed with the project.

   _____

5. We had hoped to make a decision by now, however, we are still waiting for information from the client.

   _____

ANSWERS   RUN-ON?

1. The agency completed the investigation last month; its
    findings were inconclusive.

    _____

2. We believe the problem is separate; it is not related to
    the earlier fire.

    _____X_____

3. She has received the most up-to-date-treatment, <u>but</u>
    her recovery is hindered by her depression.

    _____X_____

4. Let me know if you would like to meet with our team;
    meanwhile, we will proceed with the project.

    _____

5. We had hoped to make a decision by now; however,
    we are still waiting for information from the client.

    _____X_____

Assignment

Check your own writing samples for run-on sentences. If you find any, write the originals and revisions here. If you don't find any, go on to the next section of this lesson.

ORIGINAL

_____

_____

_____

_____

REVISION

_____

_____

_____

_____

ORIGINAL

_____

_____

_____

_____

REVISION

_____

_____

_____

_____

SENTENCES THAT ARE TOO LONG

Some sentences are too long to comprehend easily in one reading. Studies show that people generally have to read sentences of more than 28-30 words at least twice.

How many times do you have to read this sentence?

> To help Debra succeed in her present position, we recommend that she be given the opportunity to participate with the department supervisor, in meetings to be held twice a month starting in the first quarter of next year, with the specific purpose of discussing alternative work methods for processing work flow. (51)

See how much easier these shorter sentences are to follow?

> To help Debra succeed in her present position, we recommend that she be given the opportunity to participate in meetings with the department supervisor. (24) These meetings will be held twice a month starting in the first quarter of next year. (16) During these meetings, Debra and her supervisor can discuss alternative methods for processing work flow. (15)

As a general rule, keep the average length of your sentences to 17–24 words, with only one or two thoughts per sentence. If you are using technical or unusual terms, drop the count to 15–18 words.

Here's how to determine if your sentences are too long:

- Count the number of words in each of five consecutive sentences. Include small words such as *a*, *the*, *to*, etc.

- Divide the total by five.

EXAMPLE

> The Data Processing Group has failed to meet its schedules for the past six months, causing delays and confusion throughout the organization. (22) To remedy this situation, please make sure all team members follow the Data Processing Organizational Plan procedures to the letter. (20)

> The Plan, which was distributed to all the teams in November, clearly establishes objectives and priorities for all department projects. (20) The procedures it contains explain each team member's responsibilities in detail. (11) The procedures also provide steps to take in the case of problems. (12)

Here are the word counts for those five sentences:

> Words per sentence: $22 + 20 + 20 + 11 + 12 = 85$

> Average words per sentence: $85 \div 5 = 17$

Now look at one of your writing samples. Count the number of words in each of five consecutive sentences.

- ■ Write down the number of words in each sentence:

  Sentence 1: _____   Sentence 4: _____

  Sentence 2: _____   Sentence 5: _____

  Sentence 3: _____

- ■ Add the five numbers and write the total: _____
- ■ Divide the total by five and write that number: _____

If the average number of words per sentence is more than 25, pay closer attention to the length of your sentences.

Here is an easy, two-step method for revising a long sentence:

1. List the ideas.

2. Write separate sentences containing only one or two ideas. Use transitions to link the sentences.

Here's an example of a long sentence. Use the method listed on the previous page to revise it.

> I worked with a number of managers and supervisors to explore the issues which surfaced during the change process, including concerns about their own limitations, a sense of loss as a result of change, reconciliation of conflicting needs and priorities, and how to preserve their own sense of worth when everyone else seems to be moving forward. (57)

_____

_____

_____

_____

_____

Your two-step revision might look like this:

1. List the ideas.

   > I worked with managers and supervisors to explore the issues resulting from changes. The issues included

   - Concerns about their limitations
   - Sense of loss as a result of change
   - Concerns about conflicting needs and priorities
   - Ways to preserve their sense of self-worth

2. Write separate sentences containing only one or two ideas. Use transitions to link the sentences.

   > I worked with a number of managers and supervisors to explore the issues that surfaced during the change process. (19)

   > Two of the major issues concerned feelings about their own limitations and their sense of loss as a result of change. (21) In addition, they wanted to reconcile their conflicting needs and priorities. (11) Finally, they are working to preserve their own sense of self-worth when everyone else seems to be moving forward. (19)

Now try some practice.

PRACTICE

Revise this 55-word sentence into several shorter ones.

> I have enclosed a survey form that will allow you to give me feedback about the process used to set up the display booth that will help us learn whether our customers were satisfied with the arrangements and if they were not, we want to know what specific changes we should make for next year.

1. List the ideas.

    _____

    _____

    _____

    _____

2. Write separate sentences containing only one or two ideas. Use transitions to link the sentences.

    _____

    _____

    _____

    _____

    _____

    _____

    _____

    _____

    _____

Turn the page to check your revision.

Once you've listed the ideas and written out separate sentences for them, your revision should look something like this. Word counts are noted in parentheses.

> I have enclosed a survey form that will allow you to give me feedback about the process used to set up the display booth. (25) Your feedback will help us learn whether our customers were satisfied with the arrangements. (14) If they were not satisfied, we want to know what specific changes we should make for next year. (18)

Assignment

Review your own writing. Look for a sentence that is more than 24 words long. Write the original and the revision here. (If you don't find any, go on to the next section of this lesson.)

ORIGINAL

_____

_____

_____

_____

_____

_____

REVISION

_____

_____

_____

_____

_____

COMMAS

We'll review four situations when you must use a comma:

1. To set off a clause that does not change the meaning of a sentence

2. In some dates and addresses

3. To prevent misunderstanding

4. For items in a series

1. COMMAS AND CLAUSES

A clause is set off with commas if it could be removed without changing the meaning of the sentence. That rule can be restated in two ways.

First, do not set off a clause with commas if removing the clause would change the meaning of the sentence.

WITH CLAUSE   Cars <u>that have faulty brakes</u> are a menace.

WITHOUT CLAUSE   Cars are a menace.

Without the clause "that have faulty brakes," the sentence has a different meaning. Therefore, it would be incorrect to surround the clause with commas.

Second, use commas to set off a clause that does not affect the meaning of the sentence.

WITH CLAUSE   Dave's mother**,** <u>who is 57</u>**,** is visiting him in July.

WITHOUT CLAUSE   Dave's mother is visiting him in July.

In this example, removing the clause "who is 57" does not change the essential meaning of the sentence. The age of Dave's mother is irrelevant to the fact that she's visiting in July. The clause stating her age is therefore set off with commas.

On the next page you'll find some practice.

PRACTICE

Underline the clauses in these sentences. Then insert commas to set off clauses that don't change the meaning of the sentence.

1. Her e-mail which I received yesterday stated very clearly that the work was to be completed by next month.

2. Activities of our company that are directly related to this program are developed by the Processing Division.

3. Engineers who are new to this procedure should not try to carry it out themselves.

4. The report which was written by hand was submitted on time.

Check your answers on the next page.

ANSWERS

1. Her e-mail, which I received yesterday, stated very clearly that the work was to be completed by next month.

2. Activities of our company that are directly related to this program are developed by the Processing Division.

3. Engineers who are new to this procedure should not try to carry it out themselves.

4. The report, which was written by hand, was submitted on time.

---

2. COMMAS IN DATES AND ADDRESSES

In sentences, use commas to set off the year after a day of the month, and the town and state in an address. In addresses and dates, it's often necessary to use commas in pairs.

INCORRECT	She lived at 186 Elm Lane Hibbing Minnesota.
CORRECT	She lived at 186 Elm Lane, Hibbing, Minnesota.

INCORRECT	January 1 1988 was the date of the great flood.
CORRECT	January 1, 1988, was the date of the great flood.

When the date consists only of the month and year, omit the comma after the month.

He retired in June 2004.

The magazine was dated April 1996.

On the next page you'll find some practice.

PRACTICE

Add commas where they're necessary.

1. When the client died on September 28 2007 his policy was still pending.

2. We inspected the property at 230 Clark Street Novato and found that an illegal unit had been constructed.

3. She has been with the company since July 2000.

Check your answers on the next page.

ANSWERS

1. When the client died on September 28, 2007, his policy was still pending.

2. We inspected the property at 230 Clark Street, Novato, and found that an illegal unit had been constructed.

3. She has been with the company since July 2000. [*correct: no comma is necessary between the month and the year*]

3. COMMAS THAT PREVENT MISUNDERSTANDING

Some sentences sound clear in a writer's mind, but could confuse the reader. Commas are invaluable, multipurpose tools to make your meaning clear by showing the reader how you pace your thoughts.

A reader would probably be confused by the unpunctuated, rapid-paced sentences below. In each case, a comma easily clears up the confusion by showing the reader where to pause between ideas.

CONFUSING   Although there were jobs for a hundred thousands applied.

CLEAR   Although there were jobs for a hundred**,** thousands applied.

CONFUSING   In brief the report will take about an hour.

CLEAR   In brief**,** the report will take about an hour.

Turn the page for some practice.

PRACTICE

Insert commas where you think they're necessary.

>   **ORIGINAL** After all the time he has taken has been well spent.

>   **REVISION** After all, the time he has taken has been well spent.

1.   As you know nothing changed as a result of the investigation.

2.   If you want to swim the pool is a block away.

3.   To summarize case histories are the most important documents in our files.

Check your answers on the next page.

ANSWERS

1. As you know, nothing changed as a result of the investigation.

2. If you want to swim, the pool is a block away.

3. To summarize, case histories are the most important documents in our files.

4. THE SERIES COMMA

Finally, without commas, three or more items in a series can run into one another. The result can be confusing.

> Alphonse's first assignments will be to clean the shelves move the filing cabinets put the books in alphabetical order and take the outdated files to the warehouse.

Commas make it clear that each item in the series—in this case, four activities—is separate.

> Alphonse's first assignments will be to clean the shelves, move the filing cabinets, put the books in alphabetical order, and take the outdated files to the warehouse.

"Red, white, and blue" is an example of three **items in a series.** The most common conjunctions for items in a series are the words *and* and *or*.

One of the most common punctuation questions is whether to use a comma before the final conjunction in a series of three or more items. This punctuation is sometimes called the **series comma.** In fact, there is no hard-and-fast rule about including or omitting the series comma.

WITHOUT SERIES COMMA   The store has the shirt in red, blue, green and yellow.

WITH SERIES COMMA   The store has the shirt in red, blue, green, and yellow.

In most situations, you can use the series comma or omit it, as long as you *consistently* use it or omit it throughout your entire document. But you must use the series comma whenever a sentence would be confusing without it.

WITHOUT SERIES COMMA (**CONFUSING AND INCORRECT**)	The tasks our group must complete by next Wednesday include editing the brochure, preparing the mailing list and printing the labels and printing and mailing the brochures.
WITH SERIES COMMA (**CLEAR AND CORRECT**)	The tasks our group must complete by next Wednesday include editing the brochure, preparing the mailing list and printing the labels **,** <u>and</u> printing and mailing the brochures.

The series comma always goes before the conjunction, and never after it.

INCORRECT	Send the company treasurer your last three pay stubs, a copy of your federal tax return <u>and</u>**,** copies of any form 1099s you might have received.
CORRECT	Send the company treasurer your last three pay stubs, a copy of your federal tax return **,** <u>and</u> copies of any form 1099s you might have received.

SOME ORGANIZATIONS HAVE RULES ABOUT COMMA USAGE. If your organization doesn't have this kind of rule, we recommend always using the series comma before the conjunction. Then you'll never have to ask yourself whether the comma will prevent confusion, and you'll never be wrong.

**Before practicing the use of commas in a series,
take a look at the use of semicolons and colons.**

SEMICOLONS AND COLONS

Like commas, semicolons can separate items in a series. Semicolons and colons also indicate different kinds of transitions within a sentence from one clause to another.

SEMICOLONS

Here are three situations when you'd use a semicolon.

1. To separate a series of items that already contain one or more commas:

    > Four people were unable to attend the meeting: Joe Masumoto, the club treasurer; Keira Jones; Louise Boswart, the club president; and José Rodriguez.

2. To join two unrelated clauses when you don't want to use a conjunction such as *and, but,* etc.:

    > They agreed to select the lowest bidder; they had to wait ten days for the results.

3. To join two clauses with a word like *therefore, however,* etc., plus a comma:

    > We expected the report the first week of June; however, the project manager has asked for a two-week delay.

COLONS

Next, we'll look at the three most common uses for colons in business writing.

1. Use a colon after the salutation of a formal business letter:

    > Dear Ms. Young:

2. Use a colon to introduce a series of items or a bulleted list after a word or phrase like *the following*:

    > The additional materials are <u>as follows</u>:
    >
    > - business newspapers
    >
    > - trade magazines
    >
    > - instructional DVDs
    >
    > - more computers

3. Use a colon to introduce a series after a stated or implied number:

    > There are <u>three things</u> you must know about your new job: starting hours, ending hours, and vacations.

SIDE-BY-SIDE PUNCTUATION MARKS

Here are some guidelines for how punctuation marks appear beside other punctuation marks in American English.

- Don't put two periods side by side: use only one period for a sentence that ends with an abbreviation.

  We'll need to take a change of clothes, something to read, snacks, etc.

  I consulted Susan Leung, M.D.

- Tuck commas and periods inside quotation marks. Put colons and semicolons outside quotation marks.

  Their supervisor reminded them, "It's important to be on time." This reminder was unnecessary.

  Their supervisor reminded them, "It's important to be on time"; this reminder was unnecessary.

On the next page you'll find some practice involving commas, semicolons, and colons.

PRACTICE

Add colons, semicolons, or commas where they're necessary.

1. The doctor said the condition has three symptoms itching hunger and thirst.

2. There are three new team members Erin Copland pitcher Jennifer Steinblum catcher and Pat Jonas shortstop.

3. The boys walked home from practice their coach had left earlier.

4. I find the Sherwood proposition very appealing however I'd like to know more about the product before continuing.

5. She explained that the outbound train is delayed the news couldn't have been more unwelcome.

Turn the page to check your answers.

ANSWERS

1. The doctor said the condition has three symptoms: itching, hunger, and thirst.

2. There are three new team members: Erin Copland, pitcher; Jennifer Steinblum, catcher; and Pat Jonas, shortstop.

3. The boys walked home from practice; their coach had left earlier.

4. I find the Sherwood proposition very appealing; however, I'd like to know more about the product before continuing.

5. She explained that the outbound train is delayed; the news couldn't have been more unwelcome.

Up next is a section on dashes and parentheses.

DASHES AND PARENTHESES

Dashes and parentheses set off information that isn't essential to the meaning of a sentence.

Dashes call attention to information:

> Aileen has a knack for learning new computer software—even though
> she has never taken a class—and she often teaches her colleagues
> new computer skills.

And parentheses indicate that information is less important than the rest of the sentence:

> Aileen has a knack for learning new computer software (even though she has never
> taken a class), and she often teaches her colleagues new computer skills.

In that sentence, you could also use commas to set off the information about Aileen's never having taken a class. You would choose dashes to emphasize this information, and choose parentheses to deemphasize it.

DASHES

If you're setting off information that comes in the middle of a sentence, be sure to use a pair of dashes: one before *and one after* the information.

INCORRECT   As a receptionist, Miri has several good qualities—a good voice and an excellent memory, but she is sometimes rude to callers.

CORRECT   As a receptionist, Miri has several good qualities—a good voice and an excellent memory—but she is sometimes rude to callers.

But if you're setting off information that comes at the end of a sentence, only one dash is necessary:

> Mel was hoping to be given the new territory—he said that he was
> disappointed when it was assigned to Peter instead.

Never use a comma before or after a dash.

INCORRECT   I will not be able to meet with you on December 28,—our company closes down that week—,but let's try for the first week of January.

CORRECT   I will not be able to meet with you on December 28—our company closes down that week—but let's try for the first week of January.

198 PROFESSIONAL WRITING SKILLS: A WRITE IT WELL GUIDE

DIFFERENT WAYS TO TYPE A DASH

The following are a hyphen, an e<u>n</u> dash, and an e<u>m</u> dash: - – — . We've used em dashes in this book (—), but many writers now use an en dash surrounded by spaces (–). Either kind of dash is correct; just be sure to be consistent and use only one kind.

If neither kind of dash is available, it is also correct to use two side-by-side hyphens to represent a dash (--), though em or en dashes look more professional. It's incorrect to use a single hyphen surrounded by spaces (-) to represent a dash.

PRACTICE

Insert dashes into these sentences.

1. Because so many of our customers moved last year, our business dropped by 10 percent our first drop in three years.

2. Brenda is delighted with her new position it is much more challenging than her previous one and she is already preparing for her next promotion.

ANSWERS

Here is where the dashes go:

1. Because so many of our customers moved last year, our business dropped by 10 percent—our first drop in three years.

2. Brenda is delighted with her new position—it is much more challenging than her previous one—and she is already preparing for her next promotion.

PARENTHESES

Readers often skip information included in parentheses (or pay less attention to it), so save parentheses for information that is not essential to your message.

> We are requesting bids for remodeling the building on Elm Avenue (formerly Sixth Street Center).

Also use parentheses when you want to present a new acronym:

> The engineers learned how to prepare an environmental impact assessment (EIA).

For parenthetical statements that appear in the middle of a sentence, do not use a comma before the first parenthesis. You should use a comma after the closing parenthesis *only* if you would add the comma at that place if the parenthetical information were removed.

INCORRECT   We have found a graphic design service, (Elephant Graphics) that does excellent work and has reasonable prices.

INCORRECT   We have found a graphic design service (Elephant Graphics), that does excellent work and has reasonable prices.

CORRECT   We have found a graphic design service (Elephant Graphics) that does excellent work and has reasonable prices.

The third example is correct because the sentence would have no comma without the name Elephant Graphics: "We have found a graphic design <u>service that</u> does excellent work and has reasonable prices."

Here's an example of a sentence that could either include or omit a comma if the parenthetical information were removed. If the comma is included, it must follow the parentheses.

INCORRECT   After the developers finish their field tests, (their deadline is May 15) they can give us a good idea of when we can launch the system.

CORRECT   After the developers finish their field tests (their deadline is May 15), they can give us a good idea of when we can launch the system.

CORRECT   After the developers finish their field tests (their deadline is May 15) they can give us a good idea of when we can launch the system.

When parentheses set off words at the end of a sentence, the final punctuation mark goes *outside* the parentheses.

> Emmie said she would chair the committee (she says the same thing every year).

> When do you think you will complete the project (assuming all goes well)?

When an *entire* sentence is enclosed in parentheses, put the final punctuation mark *inside* the parentheses.

> You can use your telephone to listen to the radio. (You will need to purchase the optional radio headset accessory.)

> We will activate your membership on October 1. (Isn't that the start date you requested?)

Always use both opening and closing parentheses.

INCORRECT It seems likely that we will finish the project by next <u>week (as</u> long as we receive the necessary information from the <u>client, so</u> it's time to alert the Production Department to expect our draft report.

CORRECT It seems likely that we will finish the project by next week (as long as we receive the necessary information from the client), so it's time to alert the Production Department to expect our draft report.

PRACTICE

Try inserting parentheses in these sentences to deemphasize information or correct the punctuation.

1. After months of research, the journalist found the information she needed in a July 14, 2007, *New York Times* website article which she had saved on her computer, and then forgotten.

2. Anne Sumida says she will not serve as director she is hoping for a transfer to the London branch, but she is willing to take on the job until someone is hired.

3. It took us more than three weeks including two Saturdays to complete the Grady report.

ANSWERS

You could have inserted parentheses as shown below.

1. After months of research, the journalist found the information she needed in a July 14, 2007, *New York Times* website article (which she had saved on her computer, and then forgotten).

2. Anne Sumida says she will not serve as director (she is hoping for a transfer to the London branch), but she is willing to take on the job until someone is hired.

3. It took us more than three weeks (including two Saturdays) to complete the Grady report.

APOSTROPHES

Apostrophes have two primary functions: to show possession, and to take the place of missing letters when you combine words to form contractions.

EXAMPLES OF POSSESSION:

Thank you for inviting my client's manager to your presentation.

All four candidates' references were excellent.

EXAMPLES OF CONTRACTIONS:

It's [*it is*] a very interesting perspective on the problem.

We know you'll [*you will*] find our time management software very useful.

I've [*I have*] enclosed a brochure.

APOSTROPHES TO SHOW POSSESSION

Apostrophes usually show that a noun or pronoun possesses something. These apostrophes' position depends on whether the noun or pronoun is singular or plural.

When the noun or pronoun is singular, you usually show possession by adding an apostrophe + *s*.

the laptop's screen	the team's schedule
my driver's van	somebody's briefcase

Most plural nouns end in *s* or *es*. To form the possessive, place the apostrophe after the final *s*.

the students' progress	two weeks' worth of work [*not "two weeks worth of work"*]
the buses' tires	the Mitulskis' car [*for the Mitulski family as a group*]

For plural nouns that do not end in *s*, you usually indicate possession by adding an apostrophe + *s*, just as you do for singular nouns and pronouns.

the children's accounts   the women's offices

the mice's nests   the oxen's yokes

PRACTICE

Add apostrophes to these nouns and pronouns to indicate possession, as shown in the example.

EXAMPLE   one carpenters hammer

REVISION   one carpenter's hammer

the presidents office   the mens locker room

several days backlog   anyones guess

ANSWERS

These are the apostrophes you should have added:

the president's office   the men's locker room

several days' backlog   anyone's guess

These eight possessive pronouns never need apostrophes. Some of them resemble contractions that always need apostrophes (*it's*, *there's*, *who's*, and *you're*).

its	theirs	hers
his	whose	yours
ours	your	

It's important to remember that possessive pronouns already show possession—so *do not* add an apostrophe to them.

INCORRECT	The truck needs **it's** brakes adjusted.
CORRECT	The truck needs **its** brakes adjusted.

INCORRECT	This table is not **our's.**
CORRECT	This table is not **ours.**

Another common error is to add apostrophes to plural nouns that are not possessive.

INCORRECT	We plan to offer all our **customer's** a rebate.
CORRECT	We plan to offer all our **customers** a rebate.

Never add an apostrophe to a noun unless you mean to show possession.

Turn the page for some practice.

PRACTICE

To show possession, add missing apostrophes and circle incorrect ones.

1. We will test each applicants skill level.

2. My assistant never makes mistake's in entering data.

3. The refrigerator door fell off it's hinges when we opened it.

Check your answers on the next page.

ANSWERS

1. We will test each **applicant's** skill level.

2. My assistant never makes **mistakes** in entering data.

3. The refrigerator door fell off **its** hinges when we opened it.

APOSTROPHES IN CONTRACTIONS

You form a contraction by combining two words, such as "it is" and "you are." An apostrophe replaces the missing letters.

Here are the correct contractions for some common word pairs:

it is	**it's**
you are	**you're**
they are	**they're**
you will	**you'll**
cannot	**can't**
who is	**who's**
will not	**won't**

Be careful not to confuse contractions with pronouns that show possession. They may sound alike, but they're different words and are written differently.

POSSESSIVE PRONOUN	The conference table has lost **its** luster.
CONTRACTION	**It's** been a profitable year for our stockholders.
POSSESSIVE PRONOUN	Please give me **your** comments on my report.
CONTRACTION	Let me know when **you're** ready to discuss the problem.
POSSESSIVE PRONOUN	Tell your colleagues that I appreciate **their** ideas.
CONTRACTION	They will provide the information when **they're** ready.

On the next page you'll find some practice.

PRACTICE

Add apostrophes, where necessary, and circle missing apostrophes or incorrect words. Some sentences have the correct possessive forms and contractions.

1. Who's cubicle is this?

2. I told her your going; you are, arent you?

3. The plan appealed to us because of its practicality.

4. Ive been planning it for weeks.

5. Their careful work paid off. They're going to be promoted.

Turn the page to check your answers.

ANSWERS

1. **Whose** cubicle is this?

2. I told her **you're** going; you are, **aren't** you?

3. The plan appealed to us because of its practicality. [*correct*]

4. **I've** been planning it for weeks.

5. Their careful work paid off. They're going to be promoted. [*correct*]

HYPHENS

Hyphens can be as complicated as apostrophes, but there are a handful of simple rules to follow. The usual rule is to hyphenate a two-word phrase that describes a noun when the phrase comes *before* the noun. The companion rule is to use a space and no hyphen between the same two words *after* the noun.

EXAMPLES   The <u>high-end</u> merchandise sold well.

The merchandise is <u>high end</u>.

This approach also works with three-word or longer phrases, and hyphenated phrases that are split up.

EXAMPLES   They design <u>ready-to-wear</u> clothing.

Their clothing is <u>ready to wear</u>.

The <u>six-</u> and <u>seven-year-old</u> students were separated into two groups.

The students are <u>seven years old</u>.

There are two exceptions to this rule. First, don't hyphenate a two-word phrase before a noun if the first word ends in *-ly*. Do not hyphenate these *-ly* phrases after a noun, either.

EXAMPLES   Their <u>carefully phrased</u> suggestion had a good effect.

The <u>conveniently located</u> store may close next year.

The store may close next year, although it is <u>conveniently located</u>.

And second, a phrase is not hyphenated before or after a noun if it is very well known.

EXAMPLES   <u>Word processing</u> skills are required.

<u>Post office</u> prices change regularly.

Turn the page for some practice.

PRACTICE

Add hyphens, where necessary, and circle any incorrect hyphens. Each sentence may already be correct.

1. The proposal was well received.

2. It was a well received proposal.

3. The latest real estate figures are in.

4. The carefully-polished grant application impressed the foundation.

5. They saw their highest ever attendance last year.

Check your answers on the next page.

ANSWERS

1. The proposal was well received. [*correct*]

2. It was a **well-received** proposal.

3. The latest real estate figures are in. [*correct*]

4. The **carefully polished** grant application impressed the foundation. [*incorrect: no hyphen*]

5. They saw their **highest-ever** attendance last year.

Turn the page for an assignment.

Assignment

Review your own writing samples for run-on sentences and incorrect or missing commas, semi-colons, colons, hyphens, and apostrophes. If you see any errors, write the originals and revisions here.

ORIGINAL

_____

_____

_____

_____

REVISION

_____

_____

_____

_____

ORIGINAL

_____

_____

_____

_____

REVISION

_____

_____

_____

_____

ORIGINAL

_____

_____

_____

_____

REVISION

_____

_____

_____

_____

REVIEW

To review what you've learned in this lesson, answer these questions.

1. A run-on sentence contains two or more _____ that are connected incorrectly.   (174)

2. A clause is set off with commas if it could be removed _____ the meaning of the sentence.   (184)

3. Use a semicolon to join two _____ with a word such as "however," therefore," etc.   (193)

4. Use a _____ to introduce a series introduced by a phrase like *the following*, or by a stated or implied number.   (194)

5. Never add an apostrophe to a noun unless you mean to show _____ .   (205)

6. Never hyphenate two-word adverb phrases that end in _____ .   (211)

7. Hyphenate most two-word phrases when they come _____ a noun they describe.   (211)

WHAT'S NEXT?

In this lesson, you've learned how to punctuate your document with confidence. In the next section, you'll learn how to write e-mail that looks professional and gets results.

7 WRITE EFFECTIVE E-MAIL

INTRODUCTION

Now you're ready to apply the planning and writing skills you've learned in the previous lessons to a specific type of writing which is probably crucial to your work life: e-mail.

The advances in electronic communication are rapidly changing the way we work. Yet common writing challenges keep e-mail from being as productive as it could be.

People still send e-mail that is confusing, unprofessional, or offensive, or that lands them and their organizations in court. Like any other business writing, effective, professional e-mail requires thought and attention.

OBJECTIVES

This lesson will help you with the following challenges:

- Writing clear, concise e-mail that quickly conveys the information people need and gets the results you want

- Conveying a professional image of yourself and your organization through the e-mail you send

- Avoiding trouble by recognizing what topics and information are and are not appropriate

E-mail is ideal for the kinds of quick messages that most of us send in response to questions, to pass along information, and to make requests. We use e-mail because it's quick and easy—more like leaving a phone message than writing. It may not seem to take the same kind of thinking and planning time as writing a hard-copy letter, or a report.

But e-mail is still writing. Even if you have only a simple message to convey, you will get better results if you stop and think about why you're writing, what information you want to pass along, and what you want the recipient to do. Unplanned messages waste everybody's valuable time.

IS E-MAIL THE APPROPRIATE CHOICE FOR THIS MESSAGE?

What if you received the two e-mail messages below? Is e-mail the best way—or the right way—to communicate the information? Why or why not?

> Dear Daniel,
>
> This is to notify you that you have come in more than half an hour late four days out of the past seven. We spoke about this issue during your last performance evaluation. If you show up late one more time, I will be forced to institute disciplinary proceedings.
>
> Sincerely,
>
> Larissa
>
> ——
>
> Billie,
>
> I know how you feel about that invoice. I almost screamed at the finances woman when she kept telling me she didn't have it. I can't find my copy either, and I know you sent me at least two of them.
>
> Could you please fax me copies ONE MORE TIME? This will get solved today, or I start building a death-ray laser gun out of office supplies. Sorry for the tirade!
>
> By the way, I heard that your manager is thinking about leaving the company. His daughter told my daughter in gymnastics class.
>
> Better keep it to yourself, but I thought you'd like to know.
>
> Parker

You probably agree that e-mail was not the appropriate choice for either of these messages. Larissa's message to Daniel addressed performance issues, which should always remain confidential and are best addressed in person. And Parker used e-mail to vent his feelings, something he might later regret. He also passed on a rumor, assuming that Billie would keep it confidential.

Convenience is not a good-enough reason for using e-mail to communicate certain kinds of information. E-mail is too public for some messages. It's more like sending a postcard than sealing a letter into an envelope.

CONSIDER THE CONSEQUENCES

To make sure that e-mail is the appropriate choice, think carefully whenever you need to communicate

- confidential or private information
- sensitive topics
- complex information

People other than your intended recipients could always see any e-mail you send. Before clicking Send, ask yourself what might happen if someone published your e-mail draft in a newspaper.

E-mail is no substitute for a conversation, or a memo or letter, that only the recipient is likely to see. Sometimes it's easy to throw negative feelings into an e-mail and send it off without pausing to think how the recipient might react. Face-to-face interaction is vital when your message might upset other people.

The casualness of e-mail also makes it easy to forget that it can be the wrong place to poke fun at an individual or a group. Something that seems funny to you could offend others who see the message. Offensive e-mails can get you—and your organization—in a lot of trouble.

An e-mail is not the best way to convey complex information, which is hard to read on a screen and may look different in a printout. To make the document more useful for the recipient, send complex information as an attached file that describes—and perhaps summarizes—the file's contents.

THINK ABOUT . . .

Have you ever received an inappropriate e-mail? How did you feel about it? Did other people see it? Were there any consequences? Did it affect the business relationship?

In the last two weeks, have you sent e-mails with messages more appropriate to a different kind of document—or that should not have been communicated at all?

APPLYING THE SIX STEPS TO E-MAIL

Think about how you read e-mail. Do you sit back with a cup of coffee and ponder every word? Most readers are likely to read only the first few lines before deciding whether the e-mail merits any more of their time. If it does, they scan the rest of the message to pick out the important points.

> For a review of the six steps, see Lesson 1: Develop a Writing Plan in Six Steps.

This fast reading makes it all the more important to plan your document. The six steps you learned in Lesson 1 work as well for e-mail as for any other kind of document.

Remember that communication is a two-way process: your e-mail recipients must receive and be able to understand your message. Stop to think about the point of view of your e-mail recipients as carefully as you would for the readers of a letter you'd write.

When sending the same message to several people or a large group, ask yourself whether the readers' needs, interests, and concerns are similar enough for one message to be appropriate for all of them. If not, you'll get better results by writing more than one e-mail, tailored to different audiences. You might write one e-mail providing some background context for a topic, and another short e-mail to people who already know this information.

WRITING TO PEOPLE YOU DON'T KNOW

When you do not know your e-mail recipients, weigh factors like the type of organization they work for, their positions, and their relationship to you and your organization. Here are some profiles of different types of recipients.

- **Customer service representatives.** You can assume they want to be helpful, know a lot about a product but little or nothing about your specific question or complaint about it, and receive hundreds of similar messages every week.

- **Prospective clients who have asked for information about your products.** They probably know something about your business, but need details from you to decide whether your product meets their needs.

- **Managers in another area who have asked for information about a project.** They're interested in your information, probably need a summary of key points rather than small details, and may lack your technical knowledge.

Too often, we write e-mail out of habit, without thinking about why we are writing. Like any other business document, e-mail is far more clear—and gets better results—when you determine your purpose before writing.

To get the most important information across quickly and clearly for a reader skimming your e-mail, decide on your single, main point; frame it as a key sentence; and put it at the beginning. Expand on your main point with facts and ideas. As you write, stop and think about exactly what information a reader needs. For an e-mail to be useful, your information should answer all the reader's questions—and only those questions. In a document as brief as an e-mail, it's especially important to group your points into logical categories that facilitate skimming.

Together, these steps will leave the recipients of any e-mail you write with a complete, coherent message that accomplishes your purpose.

LAUNCHING YOUR MESSAGE

E-mail can save us a lot of time, but it raises concerns that don't come up in other business documents:

- How do I make sure my message conveys the right tone?
- How can I format my e-mail to be easy to read?
- Do I always have to use a salutation? A closing? Complete sentences?
- Do my punctuation and grammar have to be perfect?
- What should be on the subject line?

These questions don't have quick and easy answers. But the tips and techniques on the following pages will help you send e-mail that achieves your goals and meets your readers' needs.

READ FOR SENSE

Keep yourself in the recipient's shoes, and read through your e-mail before sending it. Make any necessary changes to the content of the message right away, before worrying about the formatting, subject line, or other components. If there is any unnecessary information, delete it. If you forgot anything essential, add it.

Stop yourself if you find yourself rewriting the message, moving things around, or adding a lot of new information. Remember your purpose, audience, and main point, and the questions the e-mail needs to answer.

When you read for sense, also check the tone. Is the e-mail too abrupt? Too casual? Too formal? Not friendly enough?

ABRUPT:	Get me the revisions by Thursday.
POLITE:	Please be sure to get me the revisions by Thursday.
POLITE:	I would appreciate your getting me the revisions by Thursday.
CASUAL:	Got a lot on my plate right now—not sure I can take on a new gig.
PROFESSIONAL:	I'm very busy at the moment, and I'm not sure I can take on a new project.
FORMAL:	Prior to July 23, payments can be sent only through the Postal Service. Subsequent to that date, payments must be made through our website.
FRIENDLY:	Before July 23, you can make payments only by mail. After July 23, you can make payments on our website.

Don't use all-capital or all-lowercase letters. They are hard to read and, respectively, sound either too demanding or too casual.

MAKE THE E-MAIL EASY TO READ

How easily can you follow this e-mail message?

Hi, Laura,

The total contribution you've made for this tax year is $7,200. The maximum contribution for the year is $11,000 plus an additional $1,000 if you are age 50 or older. If Craig wishes to contribute the maximum, he can contribute $4,800 for the rest of the year (12,000 less 7,200 = 4,800).

If he can get the Salary Reduction Agreement form to me by Tuesday we can take advantage of the last three months in this tax year (4,800 divided by 3 = $1600). Next year's maximum is $12,000 plus an additional $2,000 if age 50 or older. Our tax year begins with the December pay period (the check that's issued on January 1.) I hope this information is helpful.

Best wishes,

Pierre

Pierre clearly didn't think about how that message would look on a computer screen—or on a handheld device. Even though the message is well written, it takes effort to understand it.

Notice how much easier the message is to read when it's broken down into short paragraphs, with a blank line between each one:

> Hi, Laura,
>
> The total contribution you've made for this tax year is $7,200. The maximum contribution for the year is $11,000, plus an additional $1,000 if you are age 50 or older.
>
> If Craig wishes to contribute the maximum, he can contribute $4,800 for the rest of the year ($12,000 less $7,200 = $4,800). If he can get the Salary Reduction Agreement form to me by Tuesday, we can take advantage of the last three months in this tax year ($4,800 divided by 3 = $1,600).
>
> Next year's maximum is $12,000 plus an additional $2,000 if you are age 50 or older. Our tax year begins with the December pay period (the check that's issued on January 1).
>
> I hope this information is helpful.
>
> Best wishes,
>
> Pierre

CAN A PARAGRAPH BE ONLY ONE SENTENCE LONG?

Sure it can. One-sentence paragraphs are fine in e-mail messages, as long as the sentence communicates a complete thought.

> Mark,
>
> As you asked, I'll make the necessary changes to the project timetable and send you a revised calendar by next Friday.
>
> Deanna
>
> —
>
> Marketing Team,
>
> We've scheduled the telephone meeting for 10:30 a.m. tomorrow, May 3.
>
> Billy

If a message is clearly written and presented, the reader should be able to grasp the important information by quickly scanning it.

Keep these points in mind:

- Short sentences and paragraphs are easier to read than long ones

- Lists are easier to read than sentences and paragraphs

- Information is easier to follow when there's space between list items and paragraphs

> Use short sentences, short paragraphs, and bullet points to convey information in your e-mail. See pages 38, 43, 73, and 179–80 for more information.

SALUTATIONS

E-mail doesn't always need to follow the same rules as formal business correspondence. But a salutation or greeting is like saying "Hi" or "Hello" when you begin a conversation. It helps you

- establish a personal contact by using the reader's name

- assure readers that the e-mail is meant for them

- set the tone

Salutations or greetings can be formal or informal, depending on the situation. If you're writing to a group, sometimes all you need is "Hi" or "Hello," followed by the first line.

SHOULD I INCLUDE A SALUTATION?

You should usually use a salutation. You can leave it off when you are holding an extended back-and-forth e-mail exchange, and sometimes when you are providing a brief answer to a question. But an e-mail that begins without so much as "Hi" can seem abrupt.

Your company policy might include guidelines for determining which kind of salutation to use. Otherwise, you can use the ones that follow.

Dear Mr. Wolinsky,	Hi, Bob,	Dear Bob,	Hello, Bob,
Bob,	Dear clients,	To my clients:	Hi, team,
Hi, everyone,	Hello, associates		

COMMAS IN SALUTATIONS?

These days, people often omit the comma between the "Hi" or "Hello" and the person's name for informal salutations:

> Hi Bob,
>
> Hi, Bob,

Either form is okay. Be sure, however, to use the comma after the person's name.

You usually need a formal salutation ("Dear . . .") only for people outside your organization. But there are exceptions. If you're writing to someone who is senior to you, such as a director or chairman of the board, it might be more appropriate to use "Dear Ms. Moreno" or "Dear Director" instead of "Hi, Allison."

Are you writing to a colleague or friend? Use an informal salutation or greeting, or just begin with the person's name. It's sometimes better to use a formal salutation when you write to someone you've never met, never spoken with on the phone, or never communicated with by e-mail.

When you reply to an e-mail message, note the way the person addressed you. If the person used a formal salutation, you should probably use a formal salutation in return. When you write to someone in another country, you might want to use a formal salutation, at least when you first begin to exchange messages. People outside the U.S. tend to be more formal in business settings.

COLONS IN SALUTATIONS?

A common question is whether to use a colon after a formal salutation, the way you would if you were writing a business letter.

> Dear Mr. O'Connor:

The evolving style is to use a comma instead of a colon.

> Dear Mr. O'Connor,

Unless your organization's style guide addresses this topic, do what feels right to you.

THINK ABOUT . . .

Do you ever receive e-mail that has no salutation or greeting? Under what circumstances does that seem okay?

What kind of salutation or greeting do you normally use when you send e-mail messages? How do you make that decision?

CLOSINGS AND SIGNATURES

A closing is like the period that ends a sentence—it lets the reader know you're done. Closings can show good manners and efficiency: they let readers know they've reached the end of the message. Your signature also tells them how to reach you.

CLOSINGS

Like the salutation, the closing can be formal, informal, or casual.

Formal   Sincerely; Regards; Yours truly

Less formal   Best wishes; Warm regards; Thank you

Casual   Thanks; See you soon

Choose a salutation and a closing that complement each other. For brief messages to friends and colleagues, it can be okay to close with only your name or even your initials. But keep in mind that this kind of closing can have a rather abrupt tone:

> Parker,
>
> UPS picked up the package today. It should arrive by next Tuesday.
>
> Sheila

> —

> Thanks for the update, Brendon—will let you know if I need more details.
>
> J.

SIGNATURES

An e-mail without a signature is like a voicemail message without a name or telephone number: the assumption is that the other person knows who you are and how to reach you. But just as someone you call might not recognize your voice or have your number handy, an e-mail recipient might not recognize your e-mail address or know your number.

To avoid these problems, always include your name and number. Repeating your e-mail address in the signature can make it easier for people to find you if they're not replying immediately. And if you use more than one e-mail address, make sure that the e-mail address on the From line is the one you want people to use.

Depending on the situation and your organization's policy, also include all or some of these details:

- Your title or position

- Your company name

- A fax number

- Your office and cell numbers, if necessary

- A mailing address

- The URL for your website

WORRIED ABOUT WHETHER YOUR MESSAGE WAS RECEIVED?

If you need to know that someone received your e-mail, but you don't need a full reply, add a line requesting a reply at the beginning or the end of the e-mail. (E.g., "Please let me know that you got this message.")

PROOFREAD!

Some people believe that a professional writing style isn't important for e-mail—that the rules of grammar, punctuation, and spelling don't apply. Let's look closely at that belief. Suppose you received the following message from someone you've never met. What would be your image of the person who wrote it?

> Dear Supplier Partner:
>
> I am pleased to announce: that InfoSearch has adcepted a offer, from Online Libary, Inc. to purchase it's website. Marcus Wellenby, Onlines CEO and I have work non-stop in recent weeks to put the deal together with minimum affects for both customers and our supplier partners. This will inable the InfoSearch.com web site to contine to operate and, give it a chance to realize it's potential.
>
> I want to apologize to any of you who have had a difficulty, in contacting us while we have operated with a skeletel staff in anticipation of this transatcion. I also want to personnelly thank you. For your support and for a wonderful asociation to those of you I have the pleasure of meeting.
>
> Best Regrds,
>
> Suzanne Boyles

Chances are, you wouldn't take Suzanne's message very seriously. After all, how credible is someone who can't take the time to write a message without glaring errors, or doesn't know how?

We think error-free e-mail is important. Remember these key points:

- The e-mail you write conveys a particular image to your readers. If your grammar, punctuation, and spelling are sloppy, your image will be, too.

- Some careless writing and errors will mislead readers, or make it difficult for them to understand what you're trying to say.

Before sending out an e-mail message, do yourself and your readers a favor by proofreading it. The process doesn't take long, and it can go a long way towards promoting a positive, professional image of you and your organization.

ATTACHMENTS

Always tell your readers whenever you attach a file to your e-mail. Otherwise, they might delete, forward, or save the message before noticing the important file they needed.

It takes time to open and read an attachment. Save your readers time by telling them what the attachment is, instead of forcing them to open it just to find out. Also include a cover e-mail that clearly explains what you expect the reader to do with the attachment.

When you send attachments, consider your audience. Sometimes only your primary reader—the person named on the To line and not the people on the CC or BCC lines—needs the attachment. In those cases, you might want to send the others a separate e-mail without the attachment.

Also, if the attachment is long and complex, consider summarizing it briefly in the body of the e-mail message.

THE SUBJECT LINE

Imagine a news website without headlines. How would you know what stories you wanted to read? A well-written subject line is like the headline for a news article: it draws the reader's attention and tells the reader what the e-mail is about. The subject line gives the reader a reason to open the e-mail. It's also your first and most important opportunity to get your message across.

Notice the difference between the original and revised subject lines in the following examples:

ORIGINAL   Changes

REVISION   Health benefits will change on Dec. 1: Please enroll

ORIGINAL   Planning date?

REVISION   Planning Project: Is meeting on Apr. 2, 6, or 9?

The revised subject lines are compelling. They grab the reader's attention and provide enough information to make the reader want to read and respond to the message.

WORD SUBJECT LINES CAREFULLY. Certain words or phrases can get your message sent to the spam, or junk mail, folder, where your reader will probably never see it. Here are a few examples:

For your eyes only	Opportunity Knocks
Profit Free	Confirmation of order
Look at this!	$$!!!!

Your organization might have a list of words and phrases to avoid. Check with the people who provide you with technical support. By the way, always put something in the subject line. A blank subject line is not only useless to the recipient, it might get your message tagged as spam.

MAKE SUBJECT LINES DESCRIPTIVE AND ENGAGING. Try to use them to pique the reader's interest. The best subject lines both summarize and introduce the contents of the e-mail.

NOT DESCRIPTIVE   Budget

DESCRIPTIVE   Marketing budget increased 10%

MAKE SUBJECT LINES SPECIFIC. An effective subject line includes enough detail to distinguish it from similar e-mails. It should tell readers what the e-mail is about, and enable recipients to find the e-mail again by searching for a key word or phrase.

VAGUE   Report

SPECIFIC   Robotix computer upgrade project report

WATCH THOSE EXCLAMATION POINTS. In a misguided attempt to call attention to their e-mail messages, some writers "liven up" their subject lines with language and punctuation in the attempt to make the message seem more important than it is.

Only 3 days left to apply!

Your presence required!!

Anything with an exclamation point get your message sent to the spam folder. Furthermore, it's unfair to mislead readers by conveying a false sense of urgency. Remember the boy who cried "Wolf!" If you do it too often, no one will ever take you seriously. If a message really is urgent, your system might let you flag it or mark it in some way. Better yet, make a phone call to let the recipient know it's coming and needs immediate attention.

MAKE SUBJECT LINES CONCISE AND CLEAR. A compelling subject line gets the message across without unnecessary words or obscure abbreviations.

WORDY AND CONFUSING	This msg inclds the details abt nu mktg pln
CONCISE AND CLEAR	New marketing plan details

Change your e-mails' subject lines when the subject changes in a reply to an earlier e-mail. In a back-and-forth multireply "conversation," pay special attention to the subject line. If the focus remains on the original topic, you might not need to change the subject line. But you can mislead or confuse the reader by keeping the original subject line when a reply or series of replies changes the topic of your current e-mail.

CONSIDER THE LENGTH. Long subject lines are often truncated, especially on handheld devices. If you can't avoid a long subject line, make sure the key information appears in its first few words.

THINK ABOUT . . .

How much attention do you pay to the subject line? Do you usually stop to consider whether it accurately describes and previews the message? Can you think of a time that you forgot to change the subject line when you replied to a message but changed the topic?

Assignment

1. Check the salutations on ten recent e-mail messages you've sent and received. Are they appropriate to the situation? Too formal? Too casual? Too abrupt? How would you change them? Write three of the original salutations or greetings on the lines below. Then write the changes you'd make.

    ORIGINAL

    _____

    _____

    _____

    _____

    _____

    REVISION

    _____

    _____

    _____

    _____

    _____

2. Look at five recent e-mail messages you've sent and five you've received. Do they have useful closings and signatures? What changes would have helped?

3. Do you already have a signature file that automatically adds a signature block to your e-mail? Do you have at least one alternative signature? If so, review those files to see whether they need any changes.

    If you don't have a signature file, create at least two that would be appropriate for the different kinds of e-mail you send. Decide which signature file should be your default—the one that will be added automatically to every message unless you manually select a different one.

    If you don't know how to create a signature file, consult your Help menu or the people in your organization who provide technical support.

4. Look through a magazine or some news articles. Circle or jot down some headlines that draw your attention. Notice how the headline writer gave you a little preview of the article in those few words. Write out the best three headlines below.

    _____

    _____

    _____

5. Look at the subject lines from five e-mails you've sent and five you've received. Do they meet the criteria of a well-written subject line discussed in this chapter? If not, how could you revise them so they would be more effective? Write three of the original subject lines and their revisions below.

    ORIGINAL

    _____

    REVISION

    _____

    ORIGINAL

    _____

    REVISION

    _____

    ORIGINAL

    _____

    REVISION

    _____

6. Write effective subject lines based on these scenarios:

    Simon needs someone to volunteer to provide administrative assistance for the Heart Association project.

    SUBJECT LINE _____

Melissa can't attend the Verizon meeting on February 6, but wants someone to attend in her place and take notes.

SUBJECT LINE _____

Grisha believes that the draft of the Clorox presentation needs a lot more work.

SUBJECT LINE _____

7. Do you regularly send e-mail to groups? Review the distribution list for at least one of those groups. Add or remove addresses to make sure that the right people—and only the right people—get those messages.

RESOURCES CONSULTED AND RECOMMENDED FOR CONTINUED LEARNING

The Chicago Manual of Style. 15th ed. Chicago: University of Chicago Press, 2003.

Einsohn, Amy. *The Copyeditor's Handbook: A Guide for Publishing and Corporate Communications, with Exercises and Answer Keys*. Berkeley: University of California Press, 2006.

Fogarty, Mignon. *Grammar Girl: Quick and Dirty Tips for Better Writing*. http://grammar.quickanddirtytips.com.

Merriam-Webster's Collegiate Dictionary. 11th ed. Springfield, MA: Merriam-Webster, Inc., 2005.

Straus, Jane. *GrammarBook.com*. http://grammarbook.com.

Turabian, Kate L. *A Manual for Writers of Research Papers, Theses, and Dissertations*. 7th ed. Chicago: University of Chicago Press, 2007.

Williams, Joseph M. *Style: The Basics of Clarity and Grace*. 3rd ed. New York: Pearson Longman, 2009.

ABOUT WRITE IT WELL

Write It Well began in 1979 as Advanced Communication Designs, Inc., a training company that specialized in helping people communicate more clearly.

Our focus has always been on providing practical information, techniques, and strategies that people can use immediately. Individuals, teams, training specialists, and instructors in corporations and businesses of all sizes, nonprofit organizations, government agencies, and colleges and universities all use our books and training programs.

The Write It Well series currently includes the self-paced training workbooks *Professional Writing Skills, How to Write Reports and Proposals, Grammar for Grownups*, and *Writing Performance Reviews*. For more about our company and detailed descriptions of our publications, visit our website, www.writeitwell.com.

ABOUT THE AUTHOR

Natasha Terk is the author of *Writing Performance Reviews: A Write It Well Guide* and the co-author of *E-Mail: A Write It Well Guide.* As the president of Write It Well, she leads the firm's business operations and strategy.

Natasha holds master's degrees from the University of San Francisco and the University of Manchester, UK. She served as a program officer at the Packard Foundation and as a management consultant with La Piana Consulting, and serves on the board of the Ronald McDonald House of San Francisco.

Natasha has taught business writing at the University of California, Berkeley. She leads on-site and online webinars and workshops for clients including Hitachi Data Systems, Hewlett Packard, Granite Construction, National Semiconductor, and the Port of Oakland. Natasha gives keynote speeches and presentations on business communications at seminars and large conferences. She develops job-relevant, engaging training solutions that help people work more effectively and efficiently.